CW00381141

THE LONDON
POCKET COMPANION

Jo Swinnerton

PAVILION

A Think Book for Pavilion Books

This edition published by Pavilion Books in 2008
First published in the United Kingdom in 2004 by Robson Books
10 Southcombe Street, London W14 0RA

Imprints of Anova Books Company Ltd

Text and design © Think Publishing 2004
The moral rights of the authors have been asserted

Edited by Jo Swinnerton
The Companion team: Vicky Bamforth, James Collins,
Harry Glass, Rhiannon Guy, Emma Jones, Matthew Stadlen,
Lou Millward Tait and Malcolm Tait

Think Publishing
The Pall Mall Deposit
124–128 Barlby Road, London W10 6BL
www.thinkpublishing.co.uk

ISBN 978-1-862057-94-4

2 4 6 8 10 9 7 5 3

Printed and bound by Millenium International Printing, China

www.anovabooks.com

THE POCKET COMPANION SERIES:
COLLECT THEM ALL

The Birdwatcher's
Pocket Companion
by Malcolm Tait and Olive Tayler
ISBN 978-1-862057-97-5

The Cook's
Pocket Companion
by Jo Swinnerton
ISBN 978-1-862057-90-6

The Fishing
Pocket Companion
by Lesley Crawford
ISBN 978-1-862057-92-0

The Gardener's
Pocket Companion
by Vicky Bamforth
ISBN 978-1-862057-95-1

The Sailing
Pocket Companion
by Miles Kendall
ISBN 978-1-862057-96-8

The Traveller's
Pocket Companion
by Georgina Newbery and Rhiannon Guy
ISBN 978-1-862057-91-3

The Walker's
Pocket Companion
by Malcolm Tait
ISBN 978-1-862057-93-7

INTRODUCTION

There is always someone who needs to know when Big Ben first struck the hour, or who sold the first grapefruit in London, or what kind of fish swim past the Houses of Parliament. The same person would probably also like to know where in London they can find a spiral escalator, an audacious jumping spider and a tobacco pouch made from the skin of an albatross. If you know a person like this, you should give them this book, as it contains the answers to all these puzzles and many more.

But before you give it to them, have a browse yourself. Because then you will discover that Gandhi once lived in Bow, that the longest game of Monopoly lasted 70 days and that a vasectomy kit and a Chinese typewriter were once left behind on an Underground train. Once you know these things – and hundreds more – you will never look at London in quite the same way again.

Jo Swinnerton, Editor

YOU SAW IT HERE FIRST

The first daily newspaper in the English language and the world's oldest continuously published newspaper was the *London Gazette*. It was first published on 7 November 1665, and is still published today, nearly 340 years later. It was first called the *Oxford Gazette*, as the court had retired to London to escape the plague, but when they returned to the capital, the paper went with them and was renamed. Samuel Pepys noted its introduction in his diary:

This day the first of the 'Oxford Gazettes' came out, which is very pretty, full of news, and no folly in it.

The paper provided a mixture of government notices, trade news, business news, shipping reports and notices about royal appointments. Historic events were recorded, such as the Great Fire of London, the Battle of Waterloo and the declaration of war against Germany in 1939. Today, the *London Gazette* is published each weekday by HMSO (Her Majesty's Stationery Office), and contains such things as national statistics, legal developments and innovations, changes in state legislation, summaries of events in the Houses of Parliament, information on European government and legislation and notices of personal and corporate insolvency (which are usually the largest categories). It also carries supplements on certain occasions, such as law exam results, the Royal honours lists and Premium Bond prize draw details. Now available online, it still carries the original, slightly stern strapline: 'Published by Authority'.

BURIED IN BUNHILL FIELDS

A few of the famous names who ended up in Bunhill Fields, London's non-conformist burial ground

William Blake, poet • John Bunyan, preacher • members of the Cromwell family • Daniel Defoe, writer

MARKET DAY

London's best markets

Bermondsey	Friday	*Antiques*
Borough	Fri & Sat	*Food*
Brick Lane	Sun	*Flea market*
Columbia Road	Sun	*Flowers, plants, garden equipment*
Greenwich	Sat & Sun	*Antiques, bric-a-brac, clothes, food*
Northcote Road	Thu–Sat	*Food*
Portobello Road	Sat	*Antiques*
Spitalfields	Mon–Fri, Sun	*food, crafts, gifts; fashion on Sunday*

LOST IN LONDON

The cleaning up of the Thames in the latter years of the 1900s has made the metropolitan waterway more appealing to certain fish and mammals who would normally keep their distance. There are currently 116 species of fish flourishing in the Thames, 30 of which migrate up and down regularly, within a few feet of the Houses of Parliament. Smelt are particularly fond of Wandsworth, where they spawn below the tide mark in March, whereas dace prefer to head for Teddington. So many flounder fry (young fish) migrate through Putney each year that they turn the water grey. Sea bass also swim through Putney, while grey mullet head for Chiswick.

The Thames also attracts more exotic visitors: a dolphin was spotted in the Thames on 25 June 2001, swimming as far as Wapping, Tower Bridge and Blackfriars Bridge, and another was seen near Hammersmith in the autumn of 1999. On 13 June 2000, a porpoise gambolled in the river. A whale was discovered swimming in the Thames in January 2006, but sadly it died during the rescue attempt.

CAPITAL CONUNDRUMS

What is the colour of a banana
and the shape of an orange?
Answer on page 144

DELIVERY NOT INCLUDED

In the 1920s a Scottish conman named Arthur Ferguson, posing as a civil servant, managed to 'sell' Nelson's Column to an American tourist for £6,000. He also sold Buckingham Palace and Big Ben before moving on to the US and parting with the White House and the Statue of Liberty. The buyers were unaware that they had been conned until they tried to collect their goods.

Ferguson was not the only one to try this trick. A man named Michael Corrigan sold the Tower of London, London Bridge and 145 Piccadilly to a number of American tourists, selling some of the buildings more than once. He also once persuaded the manager of a London jeweller's shop to lend him all the shop's stock for a day to help trap a gang of thieves, with predictable results.

HOW LONG'S THAT BEEN THERE?

Some prehistoric remains that have been dug up in London

Bears	Woolwich
Buffalo	St Martin-in-the-Fields
Crocodiles	Islington
Elephants	Trafalgar Square
Lions	Charing Cross
Mammoth	King's Cross
Sharks	Brentford
Wolves	Cheapside

OLD PICTURE, NEW CAPTION

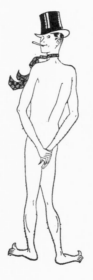

*On the first visit to his new Mayfair club, Bertie
was delighted to find there was almost nothing
that he wasn't allowed to do*

HELLO SAILOR

If you come across a sailor with a strange bulge in his
pocket, fear not; a superstition that originated in the
London docks in 1917 means that sailors used to carry
a pincushion as a charm against drowning.

WHOSE HOUSE IS THIS?

Where a few famous visitors found themselves a home in London

David Ben-Gurion (1886–1973), first Prime Minister of Israel, lived at 75 Warrington Crescent, Maida Vale, W9

Dr Edward Benes (1884–1948), President of Czechoslovakia, lived at 26 Gwendolen Avenue, Putney, SW15

Napoleon III (1808–73), French Emperor, lived at 1C King Street, St James's, SW1 in 1848

Emile Zola (1840–1902), French novelist, lived at the Queen's Hotel, 122 Church Road, Upper Norwood, SE19 from 1898–1899

Washington Irving (1783–1859), American writer, lived at 8 Argyll Street, W1

Antonio Canal (Canaletto) (1697–1768), Venetian painter, lived at 41 Beak Street, W1

Charles X (1757–1836), last Bourbon King of France, lived at 72 South Audley Street, W1 from 1805 to 1814

Jawaharlal Nehru (1889–1964), first Prime Minister of India, lived at 60 Elgin Crescent, W11 in 1910 and 1912

Mahatma Gandhi (1869–1948), philosopher and teacher, stayed at Kingsley Hall, Powis Road, E3 in 1931

Martin van Buren (1782–1862), eighth US President lived at 7 Stratford Place, W1

Vincent van Gogh (1853–1890), painter, lived at 87 Hackford Road, SW9 from 1873-74

Chaim Weizmann (1874–1952), first President of Israel, lived at 67 Addison Road, W14

The Number 11 bus is London's unofficial sightseeing bus. Its normal route takes it past the Bank of England, St Mary le Bow, St Paul's (look across the river for a view along the Millennium Bridge to the Tate Modern), Fleet Street, the Royal Courts of Justice, the Aldwych, and Somerset House. It then motors along the Strand to Charing Cross, Trafalgar Square, Whitehall (Downing Street, Horse Guards Parade), to Westminster for the Houses of Parliament and the Clock Tower, past Westminster Abbey and Westminster Cathedral, offers a view across St James's Park to Buckingham Palace, calls in at Victoria Station, then heads for Sloane Square and the King's Road, before reaching its final stop at Fulham Broadway.

The Number 11 enjoyed a moment of notoriety on Jubilee Day in 2002 when police arrested 19 anti-monarchist protesters in a pub, allegedly for breach of the peace. Short of a police vehicle large enough to hold them all, the police flagged down a Number 11, bundled the men and four other protesters on to the bus, then drove around London for two and a half hours, dropping them off at police stations around the capital. Scotland Yard praised its officers' ingenuity, but the courts disagreed. The protesters – none of whom was eventually charged – took the Met to court, and received a settlement of £80,000 and an apology.

LONDON PHRASES

London pride – a garden name for *Saxifraga umbrosa*, a hardy perennial herbaceous plant, a native of high lands in Great Britain. (b) A name anciently given to the Sweet William. Also known as none-so-pretty and St Patrick's Cabbage.

SIGNIFICANT STATUES

Nelson's Column

When Admiral Nelson was mortally wounded by
a musket ball at the Battle of Trafalgar in 1805, he
might have been gratified to know that a statue of
him would remain for ever at the heart of London, in
a square named after his last battle. In Trafalgar Square
stands Nelson's Column, which measures 185 feet high,
including the 18-foot statue of Nelson. The bronze relief
sculptures around the base are made out of captured
French cannons and depict the Admiral's victories at
Copenhagen, the Nile and Cape St Vincent as well as
Trafalgar. Nelson's remains are buried in St Paul's
Cathedral, and his monument includes a stirring call
to prayer that he wrote before the Battle of Trafalgar,
as the enemy approached. Some say that the reason he
faces south is to watch over his fleet of ships on top of
the Mall lampposts.

IT'S RENT DAY AGAIN

Every year, a strange and
very ancient ceremony is
enacted at the High
Court on the Strand. Called
the Horseshoe and Faggott
Cutting Ceremony, it
recreates the payment due
for rent on two pieces of
land. For the first, the
City Solicitor presents two
hazel rods to the Queen's
Remembrancer, who replies
'Good service,' which set-
tles the rent on the Moors
at Eardington in Shropshire.
Then a second payment is
made in the form of six
horseshoes and 61 nails, to
which the Remembrancer
replies 'Good number.' This
is the rent for the land on
which Australia House now
stands. It is not a public ceremony, though one can
apply to watch; and no one
is entirely sure if the rent
paid is the right amount , as
it was all a long time ago.

WHEN TERMINAL MEANS TERMINAL

The London Necropolis Railway was a dedicated train line that once carried the deceased to their final resting-place at Brookwood Cemetery. When the cemetery and railway opened in 1854, there were objections to dead bodies being transported in such an undignified manner, but it was thought the only practical way for the coffins to make the 25-mile journey from London. The trains began their journey at the London Necropolis Station, the entrance to which still exists at 121 Westminster Bridge Road. When the trains neared Brookwood's mainline station, they had to reverse discreetly into the cemetery termini: South Station for the Anglican coffins and North Station for the nonconformists. Mourners could accompany the bodies on the train to the cemetery, although the train company, somewhat insensitively, sold one-way tickets only. The London Necropolis Railway operated until its Waterloo terminal was bombed in 1941, after which service was never resumed.

MADE IN LONDON

Edmund Halley was the first Astronomer Royal at Greenwich, and the first person to **calculate a comet's orbit**. He predicted that a comet seen in 1682 would reappear in 1758. Sadly he died before he saw it proved, but it did reappear on cue and was named after him.

CLASSICAL LONDON WORKS

'Cockaigne (in London Town)', *Edward Elgar*
'In Honour of the City of London', *William Walton*
'A London Overture', *John Ireland*
'A London Symphony', *Ralph Vaughan Williams*

POPULATION STATISTICS

London statistics from the 2001 census

- Number of male residents: 3,468,793
- Number of female residents: 3,703,298
- Number of residents aged 15 and under: 1,448,236
- Number of residents aged 15–74: 5,300,332
- Number of residents aged 75 and over: 423,523
- The most populated age band is 30–34: there were 696,005 residents in this age band
- The most populated age band for men was 30–34 (341,087); for women it was 25–29 (360,393)
- There were 37,267 people aged 90 and over living in London
- There were 2,359,932 single people living in London (who have never been married)
- There were 2,386,210 married or remarried people living in London
- There were 1,046,888 people living alone in London
- 31,960 households didn't have their own bath, shower or toilet
- 522,471 households were living in overcrowded premises
- 5,229,187 of London's residents were born in the UK
- The largest religious group was Christian (4,176,175)

A TRIP DOWN CAREY STREET

'To be in Carey Street' was a popular euphemism for being in financial trouble. Carey Street, a small street behind the Royal Courts of Justice, has been home to the Bankruptcy Court since 1840, so there was a good chance that anyone walking down it was already in the red. The Seven Stars Pub, which opened in 1602, is one of very few buildings in central London to have survived the fire of 1666 and is still serving a consoling pint to anyone down on their luck.

RIOTING IN THE STREETS

Black Monday was the name given to 8 February 1886, when workers made redundant by the closure of the sugar refineries gathered in Trafalgar Square to protest. The protest was backed by the Conservative Association, but taken over by the Social-Democratic Federation. Ten thousand people marched along Pall Mall and threw objects at the Reform Club, as its members appeared at the windows to see what was going on. Although the SDF leaders were acquitted, the march caused chaos in London for several weeks.

CAPITAL CONUNDRUMS

Who buried his wine and a Parmesan cheese in his garden, to save them from the Great Fire of London?
Answer on page 144

LONDON'S FIRST THEATRES

The earliest London theatres opened on the South Bank, then a seedy and dangerous place. But as theatregoing became more respectable, new playhouses began to open north of the river. These were the first:

1660	Lincoln's Inn Theatre, Portugal Street WC2
1663	Drury Lane Theatre, Drury Lane WC2
1683	Sadler's Wells, Rosebery Avenue EC1
1732	Covent Garden Theatre, Covent Garden WC2
1771	Lyceum, Wellington Street WC2
1806	Adelphi, Strand WC2: originally called the Sans Pareil
1821	Theatre Royal, Haymarket WC2
1837	Almeida, Almeida Street N1
1868	Gaiety Theatre, Strand WC2: had England's first electric lighting system in 1878

LONDON'S FESTIVALS, PARADES AND SHOWS

New Year's Day Parade, *January*
10,000 performers from countries all over the world parade from Parliament Square to Piccadilly.

Chinese New Year, *January*
Chinatown hosts tourists and residents alike, with music, dancing, fireworks and food stalls, from Soho to Trafalgar Square.

Oxford and Cambridge Boat Race, *March*
Seventeen minutes of frantic rowing for the teams; a whole day of drinking for the spectators.

Flora London Marathon, *April*
World-record holders compete with charity runners in fancy dress along the 26 mile course.

Chelsea Flower Show, *May*
Garden design, plants and outdoor furniture and fierce competition in the heart of Chelsea.

Beating Retreat, *May*
Colourful military parade attended by the Queen and followed by a military band concert performed by the Massed Bands of the Household Division.

Royal Academy Summer Exhibition, *June*
Huge exhibition of semi-professional works of art.

Trooping the Colour, *June*
Stirring military parade in celebration of the Queen's official birthday.

Hampton Court Palace Flower Show, *July*
Larger and less posh than Chelsea, a superb flower show in an equally superb setting.

BBC Henry Wood Promenade Concerts, *July-September*
Series of classical concerts at the Royal Albert Hall, famous for its noisy and rumbustious Last Night of the Proms.

Notting Hill Carnival,
August
Loud and colourful,
celebration of Afro-
Caribbean culture, with
floats, parades, food and
DJs on every corner.

Thames Festival, *September*
The end of the Coin Street
Festival, with illuminated
procession and river events.

London Open House,
September
An opportunity to see
inside some of London's
most historic buildings.

Lord Mayor's Show,
November
Huge procession from
Guildhall to Waterloo
Bridge, led by the mayor in
his State coach.

CANARY WHARF FACTS

Facts and figures about 1 Canada Square, better known as the Canary Wharf Tower

- It is 244 metres high, the tallest building in Britain.
- It has 50 floors.
- 90,000 square feet of Italian and Guatemalan marble were used in the lobby.
- It has 3,960 windows.
- There are 4,388 steps.
- It has 32 passenger lifts divided into four banks, each serving a different section of the building.
- It also has two freight lifts and two firemen's lifts.
- It takes 40 seconds for the lift to ascend from the lobby to the 50th floor.
- 27,500 metric tonnes of British Steel and 500,000 bolts were used in the construction of the tower.
- The exterior walls are clad by 370,000 square feet of stainless steel.
- The aircraft warning light at the very top of the tower flashes 40 times a minute, 57,600 times a day.
- Over 80,000 deliveries are made to the loading bay of the tower every year.

On hearing that London was hosting the 2012 Olympics, Arthur stepped up his training regime

CRIME PECULIER

In 1952 a Nigerian visitor to London was accused of committing an indecent act with a pigeon in Trafalgar Square. As the law at the time prevented only indecency with an animal, the defence attempted to put the case that a pigeon was not an animal. The judge disagreed. The accused was fined £50, and a further £10 for taking the pigeon home and eating it for dinner.

SIGNIFICANT STATUES

Cleopatra's Needle

Cleopatra's Needle is an unlikely piece of history to find on the banks of a river in an English city. The obelisk, made of pink granite that was quarried in Syene, is one of a pair that once stood in front of the temple of Heliopolis, where Moses was born. Erected in Egypt around 1500 BC, the hieroglyphics in its surface were carved in praise of Pharaoh Thothmes III, and later of Rameses the Great. It was moved to Alexandria, Cleopatra's royal city, after her death, in 12 BC.

The obelisk was offered by the Viceroy of Egypt to the British people in 1819, after Nelson's victory over the French in the Battle of the Nile in 1798. However, it was left to languish in the Alexandrian sands for 70 years before General Sir James Alexander arranged to have it transported to England. Encased in an iron cylinder, it was abandoned during a storm at the Bay of Biscay, but later recovered and brought to London. The plaques around the base tell this story, and commemorate the men who died in the transportation of the stone. The bronze lions that flank it are more Victorian than Egyptian, but provide a suitably grand setting. In 1917 it gained the unfortunate distinction of being the first London monument to be hit in an air attack during World War One; a bomb exploded nearby and the plinth and the right-hand lion suffered shrapnel damage, which is still visible in a series of pockmarks in the stone and bronze.

But the 68.5-foot monolith holds a further historical secret; its plinth contains historical items such as a full set of British Empire coins, Imperial weights and measures, Bibles in various languages, a railway guide and copies of newspapers from 1879, the year in which it was erected on the Embankment.

LONDON LEGENDS

George Peabody

The name Peabody is familiar on both sides of the Atlantic thanks to a generous American whose substantial fortune has provided housing for unfortunate Londoners for hundreds of years. George Peabody was a successful merchant and banker in the US before he moved to London to continue his profession, where he soon amassed a fortune. Part of it was spent creating art galleries, libraries and museums in the US, but he was so appalled by the slums of London that he also gave $2.5 million to fund the building of flats for the impoverished, which continue today as the Peabody Trust. He was the first American to be given the freedom of the city, and a vast crowd attended his funeral in London. His Trust still provides 19,500 homes, there are 30 references to his name in the index of the A–Z and he is commemorated by a statue in Threadneedle Street.

ROYAL TOMBS IN WESTMINSTER ABBEY

Elizabeth I • Mary I • Edward the Confessor
Henry VII • James I • Edward VI • George II
Henry III • Edward I • Edward III • Richard II
Henry V • Anne • Charles II • William III
Mary II • Mary Stewart

LONDON OLYMPICS (1908 AND 2012?)

The London Olympics in 1908 proved to be the country's most successful in Olympic history. That year, UK athletes won a total of 142 medals: 56 gold, 51 silver and 35 bronze. They stand fourth in the league table of most successful countries at a single Olympic competition, surpassed only by the USA in 1904 and 1984, and the USSR in 1980, who won 242, 174 and 195 medals respectively.

ALAS, POOR EMANUEL...

In March 1978, Sotheby's of London auctioned the skull of Swedish scientist and mystic Emanuel Swedenborg, which went to a Swedish bidder for $3,200. The skull had been stolen by an amateur phrenologist, then turned up a century after Swedenborg's death in an antique shop in Wales, where it was bought by one of his heirs before being offered for auction.

WHEN A MAN IS AFRAID OF LONDON...

A few phobias that might keep you out of the city

Acousticophobia ....Fear of loud noises
Agoraphobia ....Fear of open spaces or of being in crowded, public places or leaving a safe place
Amathophobia ....Fear of dust
Anthropophobia or Sociophobia ....Fear of people or society
Aphenphosmphobia ....Fear of being touched
Automysophobia ....Fear of being dirty
Bacteriophobia ....Fear of bacteria
Batophobia ....Fear of heights or being close to high buildings
Enochlophobia ....Fear of crowds
Hodophobia ....Fear of road travel
Kainophobia ....Fear of anything new
Mechanophobia ....Fear of machines
Ophthalmophobia ....Fear of being stared at
Ornithophobia ....Fear of birds
Phengophobia ....Fear of daylight
Potamophobia ....Fear of rivers or running water
Siderodromophobia ....Fear of trains or train travel
Stenophobia ....Fear of narrow things or places
Suriphobia ....Fear of mice
Xenophobia ....Fear of strangers or foreigners

PUB QUIZ

Who drank here?

Holly Bush,
Holly Mount NW3
Customers: Samuel
Johnson, Charles Lamb

The Angel,
Bermondsey Wall SE16
Customers: Samuel Pepys,
Captain Cook

Fitzroy Tavern,
Charlotte Street
Customers: George Orwell,
Thornton Wilder, Dylan
Thomas, Cyril Connolly

Museum Tavern,
Great Russell Street, WC1
Customers: Karl Marx and
Dylan Thomas

Seven Stars,
Carey Street WC2
Early seventeenth century.
Charles Dickens once
drank here.

The Dagger, Aldersgate
Customer: Ben Jonson
(as mentioned in *The
Alchemist*)

Spaniard's Inn,
Spaniard's Road NW3
Customers: Percy Bysshe
Shelley, John Keats, Lord
Byron, Charles Dickens.
Dick Turpin stayed here
and there is a dedicated
Dick Turpin room.

Prospect of Whitby,
Wapping Wall, E1
Dates back to time of
Henry VIII; customers
included Samuel Pepys,
Rex Whistler, Judge
Jeffries and a variety
of thieves and smugglers

Assembly House,
Kentish Town Road NW5
Customer: TS Eliot

ART BY THE YARD

Sir James Thornhill who painted the beautiful interior of
the Painted Hall at the Royal Naval College in Greenwich
between 1707 and 1726, was paid £3 per square yard for
the ceiling and £1 per square yard for the walls.

MONET IN LONDON

Paintings of London by Claude Monet

Houses of Parliament, London 1905
Sun Breaking Through the Fog, Houses of Parliament,
London 1904
The London Harbour
Houses of Parliament at Sunset, London, 1903
The Waterloo Bridge, London 1903
Waterloo Bridge at Dusk, London 1904
Waterloo Bridge at Sunset, London, 1904

STEADY, VICAR

The Reverend Henry Bate (1745–1824) was as far removed from a religious man as can be imagined, and in fact for many years seemed to make his living by starting fights. While working as the editor of the *Morning Post*, he once picked a fight with a passer-by in Vauxhall Gardens for giving his female companion an inappropriate look. He insulted the stranger and challenged him to a duel. The victim roped in a friend to help, and a physical disagreement ensued in the Turk's Head Coffee House in Beak Street, which Bate won. He wrote about it in his own newspaper and was so gratified by the instant rise in circulation that he took to provoking fights with notable men, so that the resulting coverage would sell more newspapers. When one such incident backfired, Bate's proprietor, a Mr Richardson, warned him to be more careful, at which Bate accused him of spinelessness, Richardson challenged him to a duel, and Bate subsequently shot him in the arm. Bate gave up brawling for playwriting, with little success in the West End, and eventually became a London magistrate before finally retiring to Essex.

On 3 September 1878 at 6.15pm, a ferry called the *Princess Alice* set off on her journey to London. A band played on board and the passengers danced, unaware that the captain had left the helmsman behind and replaced him with someone less experienced. So when the *Princess Alice* found herself on a collision course with the 890-ton *Bywell Castle*, no one knew what to do. The rule was to pass port to port; but another rule said that pleasure ferries should keep to the southern shoreline. The *Princess Alice* chose the latter, which put the ships starboard to starboard. Within seconds the two ships had collided, and the water was filled with terrified passengers. Some were pulled out, but many were weighed down by their heavy Victorian clothing, and within 20 minutes of the accident, there was no one left alive. Of the estimated 750 passengers, only about 100 survived.

YOU LIVE... WHERE?

While residents may occasionally be baffled by the names given to roads in London, they should be grateful they did not live there in the thirteenth century. Back in 1230, Grub Street was known as Grope Lane, which in turn was a shortened version of its full and rather too literal title of 'Gropecuntelane'. The reason was that the street was part of the Southwark red-light district, otherwise known as the 'stews'. This street name was in fact found in several British cities at the time, although out of sensitivity for the gentle reader the remaining examples have not been listed here. Enquire at your local library. However, similarly named streets have been renamed Magpie Lane in Oxford, Host Street in Bristol and Grape Street in York, which is much nicer.

OLD PICTURE, NEW CAPTION

Harold was always happy to oblige the tourists with a spirited demonstration of the Lambeth Walk

FLYING FISH

In February 2004, the Environment Agency was faced with the task of explaining why an Amazonian red-bellied piranha dropped out of the sky and landed on the deck of the Thames Bubbler barge at Halfway Reach in Dagenham, east London. The Agency had to assume that someone had released their pet piranha into the river, which would have died from cold almost immediately. It is thought a seagull then picked up the 10cm-long fish and dropped it, as there were seagull beak marks in its skin. It is not known who was more surprised; the workers on the barge or the seagull.

OLD PICTURE, NEW CAPTION

The Pheasants' Revolt

CAPITAL CONUNDRUMS

Which five thoroughfares meet at Piccadilly Circus?
Answer on page 144

SEX ON STAGE

Before Mary Whitehouse was Lady Birdwood, a self-appointed moral guardian who bestowed a dubious fame upon the writer and actor John Bird. In 1970, Mr Bird wrote a play called *Council of Love*, which was produced at the Criterion Theatre. The fact that God, Jesus and the Virgin Mary were represented on stage was bad enough for Lady Birdwood, but she was further outraged that the Pope was shown with his cardinals indulging in orgies with naked women during the celebration of Mass. She invoked the 1376 Blasphemy Act against Ms Fazan, the play's choreographer and the only person involved that Lady Birdwood could find to prosecute. Had she been convicted, Ms Fazan could, according to the law, have been burned as a white witch. Fortunately the court felt that she could not be held responsible and the case was dismissed.

PAY UP ALL YE WHO PASS

This list of charges for the tollgate at Alleyn's College of God's Gift in Dulwich remains on display, although the toll is no longer charged:

For every motor car, motorcycle or motorcycle combination	6d
For every van, lorry or other commercial vehicle under one tonne laden weight	6d
For every van, lorry or other commercial vehicle from one to five tonnes laden weight	2/6
For every horse, mule or donkey not drawing	3d
For every horse, mule or donkey drawing any vehicle	6d
For beasts per score and so on in proportion for any less number	10d
For sheep, lambs or hogs per score in proportion (but not less than 1/2d) for any less number	21/2d

THE LONDON GROUP

Formerly known as the Fitzroy Group and the Camden Town Group, the London Group, formed by Walter Sickert, brought together many major painters of the era

Robert Bevan	1865–1925	*English*
Jacob Epstein	1880–1959	*American (became British)*
Harold Gilman	1876–1919	*British*
Charles Isaac Ginner	1878–1952	*French*
Spencer Gore	1878–1914	*English*
Duncan Grant	1885–1978	*English*
Augustus John	1878–1961	*British*
Wyndham Lewis	1882–1957	*Canadian/British Writer/Painter*
Henry Lamb	1883–1960	*English*
James Bolivar Manson	1879–1945	*British*
Lucien Pissarro	1863–1944	*French*
Walter Richard Sickert	1860–1942	*British*

A LOAD OF BOLLARDS

London is full of bollards. Those erected in Georgian times were mostly made from disused cannons, with a defunct cannonball blocking the mouth, in the reverse process to melting down iron railings to make weapons. Examples can be seen in India Street in EC3 and at the end of Old Barge House Alley in Blackfriars. Many bollards date from just after the Battle of Waterloo, such as the ones marked Sommers Town in Pancras Road, and others marked Clink and either 1812 or 1825, which were made by the Clink Pavement Company. The bollards in the Strand are shaped like rockets, the Imperial War Museum has bollards shaped like shells and those in Cavendish Court W1 have an almost phallic appearance.

WATCH OUT, BEADLES ABOUT

To ensure that proper behaviour was observed in his
upmarket shopping mall, Burlington Arcade, Lord George
Cavendish created his own corps of bouncers, known as
the Burlington Arcade Beadles and recruited from his own
regiment of the 10th Hussars. The Beadles' job when the
arcade opened in 1819 was to uphold decorum under its
elegant arches, which meant no singing, humming, running, dancing or opening umbrellas – rules they continue
to enforce to this day, while dressed in the original uniform
of Edwardian frock coats and gold-braided top hats.

TUBE MANNERS

Ten things to avoid doing on the Tube,
as seen by regular passengers

- Singing to your CD or MP3 player (we can hear you)
- Nodding your head vigorously in time to the music (we
  can see you)
- Thinking that because you are wearing headphones this
  also makes you invisible and starting to pick your nose
  (we can still see you)
- Watching porn on your laptop, which you downloaded
  last night (we can see you, and we'd really rather not)
- Glaring at passengers every time they shift slightly in
  their seat, because you think it means they are getting
  off at the next stop, and you want to sit down
- French kissing
- Talking to someone who doesn't want to talk to you
- Having a pee at the end of the carriage (obviously, that's
  better than doing it in the middle of the carriage)
- Sitting on the outside seat and then looking irritated
  when someone squeezes past you to get to the empty
  window seat
- Throwing up without warning. Or even with warning.

LONDON LEGENDS

Pearly Kings and Queens

The Pearly Kings and Queens are one of London's best-known eccentric traditions, although they are still a mystery to many of the city's residents. The tradition began in the late nineteenth century with Henry Croft, an orphan, who walked the streets collecting money for charity in between his road-sweeping job. It was the custom for many street traders to sew a few pearl buttons on his suit, so to attract attention, Croft covered his clothes in buttons, and found that his takings increased. He recruited a few friends to do the same, and the charity was born.

The first real Pearly society was formed in 1911, in Finchley, and became a close-knit community. When Croft died in 1930, 400 Pearlies turned out to mourn him and the event was covered by Pathe News. Since then the Pearlies have developed their own dynasty, comprising many kings and queens, each ruling over their own patch, from Clapton to Westminster. Unfortunately, like the real Royal Family, feuds and fallings-out are commonplace. In the Original London Pearly Kings and Queens Association, the word 'original' speaks volumes. In 2001, Pat Jolly, the Pearly King of Crystal Palace, defended the Pearly Queen of Harrow against charges of mishandling the books and was thrown out of the organisation for his pains. So he set up a breakaway movement called the London Pearly Kings and Queens Society. There is also another group of breakaways, the Pearly Guild. The Association is based at St Martin's, the Society at St Paul's and the Guild at St Mary-le-Bow, and despite their differences, all three work tirelessly through the year, raising money for London charities.

LET THEM EAT CAKE

On 5 January every year, the cast and crew of the
Theatre Royal Drury Lane eat Baddeley Cake in memory
of Richard Baddeley, a successful actor. On his death in
1794, he left a sum of money in his will to provide a
cake for Twelfth Night every year, as well as wine to drink
with it. So as not to invite bad luck, the theatre still
maintains the tradition, and the cake is duly eaten
every year on 5 January. It is carried into the Green Room
by attendants wearing eighteenth century costume, and
the company drinks to the health of their benefactor.

BRIDGE OVER TROUBLED WATERS

Blackfriars Bridge has a long history, but is perhaps most
famous for being the execution site of Roberto Calvi, found
hanging under the bridge on 18 June 1982, with his pockets
full of bricks. No one was convicted of his murder, but it
was widely rumoured that the Sicilian Mafia were taking
their revenge on the unfortunate banker, as he had lost
some money that he borrowed from them to bail out the
bank of which he was chairman. Five people were acquitted
of murdering Calvi, known as 'God's Banker', in 2005.

NOW PLEASE WIPE YOUR FEET

Seven superb footscrapers to be seen in London

At **28 Meadway, NW11** – complete with horse
At **30 Chester Street** – two squatting toads
At **36A Elvaston Place** – hemispheric, double-ended and
with added finials
Outside **St Paul's at The Ridgeway, NW7**
– with dolphin tails
At **12 Blenheim Road, NW8** – with dragon's wings
At **2 Cheyne Row, SW3** – a slightly disdainful face mask

INMATES OF NEWGATE PRISON

Moll Cutpurse (Mary Frith), highwaywoman

Daniel Defoe, author, for publishing a satirical pamphlet

Sir Thomas Malory, author of *Le Morte d'Arthur*,
for murder

Titus Oates, imprisoned for falsely claiming that there
was a Catholic plot to assassinate Charles II

Jack Sheppard, burglar, immortalised in
The Beggar's Opera

Jonathan Wild, Thief-Taker, for being over-zealous
in his duties

MADE IN LONDON

Hiram Maxim invented the **automatic machine gun** in his
workshop in Hatton Garden. Patented in 1883, it could
fire up to 600 rounds a minute. He also invented a loco-
motive headlight and a set of curling tongs, among 100
other ideas.

LEFT LUGGAGE

In October 1953, Dylan Thomas left his handwritten
manuscript – the only copy – for *Under Milk Wood*
in the Admiral Duncan pub on Old Compton Street in
Soho shortly before he left the country, promising that
whoever found it could keep it. His promise sparked
off a bizarre treasure hunt, and the manuscript was
eventually tracked down by BBC producer Douglas
Cleverdon, who later sold it for £2,000. Sadly, the
Admiral Duncan is more likely to be remembered for
another parcel that was left there in April 1999, a nail
bomb, which killed three people and injured many more.

London's first major fire was in AD 60, when the warrior queen Boadicea burned the city to the ground. Boadicea was the queen of the Iceni, the tribe that occupied East Anglia, but which was under Roman jurisdiction, and subject to conscription and heavy taxes. When Boadicea's husband, King Prasutagus, died, he left most of his wealth and estate to the Emperor Nero, but retained a small part of it for his wife and two daughters. But the Romans decided to take all of it, and when Boadicea protested, they took her prisoner and flogged her and raped her two daughters. The women escaped and returned to their home, and had soon raised an army of over 100,000 men and women to avenge the Queen's treatment and reclaim England from the Romans. They marched on the Roman strongholds of Colchester, London and St Alban's, and burned the last two to the ground. In London, the fires were so fierce that they left, buried deep beneath a part of the City, a geological layer known as Boadicea's Layer, a chunk of red band of fired clay and debris.

Boadicea was not merciful; any Britons loyal to the Romans met a horrible and bloody end. The warrior queen defeated the Romans in several confrontations, but were eventually beaten on the island of Anglesey, in a battle in which over 80,000 Britons were slaughtered. Boadicea survived the battle but chose to poison herself rather than fall into the hands of the Romans. A bronze statue of her stands on Victoria Embankment, erected in 1850.

CAPITAL CONUNDRUMS

What is unusual about the waiters at Pratt's?
Answer on page 144

THE DAY THE MUSIC DIED

Nine musicians who met their end in London

Marc Bolan
16 September 1977
The lead singer with T-Rex crashed into a tree on Barnes Common.

Graham Bond
8 May 1974
The founder member of the Graham Bond Organisation fell under a tube train at Finsbury Park.

Sandy Denny
21 April 1978
Fairport Convention's former lead singer died of a cerebral haemorrhage after falling down a flight of stairs a month earlier.

Jimmy McCulloch
27 September 1979
The guitarist with Wings was found dead in his London flat, allegedly of a drug-related heart failure.

Jimi Hendrix
18 September 1970
Hendrix died on arrival at St Mary Abbots Hospital after choking on his own vomit as the result of a barbiturates overdose.

'Mama' Cass Elliot
29 July 1974
The generously sized singer from the Mamas and Papas died of a heart attack.

Pete Farndon
14 April 1983
The Pretenders' guitarist died of a drug overdose.

Keith Moon
7 September 1978
The drummer with The Who died in his sleep after an overdose of anti-seizure medication, rather than of the recreational drugs that were first suspected.

THE MUSICAL DICTATOR

Italian dictator Benito Mussolini so enjoyed the song 'The Lambeth Walk' from the 1937 musical *Me and My Girl* that he engaged a London girl to travel to Italy to teach it to him.

OLD PICTURE, NEW CAPTION

*An unsuspecting tourist discovers how much
it will cost to be driven south of the river*

TILL DEATH US DO PART?

When the first wife of Martin van Butchell died in 1775, van Butchell declined to bury his poor wife and instead had her embalmed, fitted with glass eyes and displayed, wearing her wedding dress, in a glass case at his home in Mayfair. But unless this be mistaken for an act of love by a husband who could not bear to be parted from his wife, it should be noted that her considerable fortune was bequeathed to a distant relative, to be paid as soon as she was 'dead and buried'. Van Butchell also charged visitors to see her body. In 1815 after van Butchell's death, his son donated the embalmed body to the Royal College of Surgeons, where it was eventually destroyed by a German bomb in 1941.

SPORTING LONDON

The Oxford and Cambridge Boat Race was begun in 1829 when two school friends from Harrow challenged each other to a boat race: Charles Merivale and Charles Wordsworth (nephew of William), who were studying at Cambridge and Oxford respectively. The first race took place in Henley-on-Thames on 10 June 1829, and was won by Oxford (after a restart). Twenty thousand people turned out to watch, which inspired the townsfolk to begin their own annual event, the Henley Royal Regatta. The boat race relocated to Westminster in 1836, then to Putney in 1845 when Westminster became too crowded. It became an annual event in 1856, and was rowed from Putney to Mortlake.

Since then, the race has become a treasured national event, attracting enormous crowds and television viewing figures of nearly nine million people. And every year's broadcast revisits the statistics of previous years, including:

- the first sinking took place in 1859, when Cambridge sank; in 1912 both crews sank and the race was re-run the following day. Oxford first sank in 1925.
- the BBC broadcast a running commentary for the first time in 1927; the race was first televised in 1938.
- in 1976, Oxford became the first team to complete the course in under 17 minutes.
- the fastest time to date was set by Cambridge in 1998, when they finished in 16 minutes and 19 seconds.
- in 1981, Sue Brown became the first woman to take part, as cox for Oxford.
- the closest finish was in 2003, when Oxford won by a mere foot; the 1877 contest was recorded as a dead heat, but the measuring equipment was unsophisticated and it is thought that Oxford in fact won by six feet.
- the current tally of wins over 153 races is Cambridge 79, Oxford 73, plus one dead heat.

HERE TODAY, GONE TOMORROW

The *London Daily News* had possibly the shortest career of any UK newspaper. Launched on 24 February 1987 by the ebullient Robert Maxwell, it closed on 23 July the same year. Maxwell, who was by then owner of the Mirror Group, wanted his new rag to be the first 24-hour newspaper in Britain and cheaper than all its rivals. But Associated Newspapers, publishers of the *Daily News*'s competitor, the *Evening Standard*, fought back and undermined Maxwell's attempt by relaunching the defunct *Evening News* at an even lower price. Maxwell was forced to admit defeat. It is estimated that the exercise cost him some £50 million.

LONDON, WHERE?

A few US towns that sound familiar...

London, *Arkansas*
London, *Arizona*
London, *California*
London, *Kentucky*
New London, *Minnesota*
New London, *Missouri*
New London, *New Hampshire*
New London, *North Carolina*
London, *Ohio*
London, *Oregon*
New London, *Pennsylvania*
London, *Texas*
London, *West Virginia*

LONDON PHRASES

London clay – a geological formation in the lower division of the Eocene in SE England.

RIOTING IN THE STREETS

The first Bloody Sunday took place on 13 November 1887, when the Social Democratic Federation organised a meeting in Trafalgar Square to protest against the government's policies. The police were ordered to stop the demonstration, and advanced on the crowd. Onlookers were shocked at the police violence. One commented: 'To keep a crowd moving is, I believe, a technical term for the process of riding roughshod in all directions, scattering, frightening and batoning the people.' Two people were killed and 200 were injured.

THE 21 TOWERS OF LONDON

The Tower of London is made up of 21 towers, 20 of which are still standing:

Beauchamp • Bell • Bloody • Bowyer • Brick
Broad Arrow • Byward • Constable • Cradle
Devereux • Develin • Flint • Lanthorn
Martin • Middle • Salt • St Thomas's
Wakefield • Wardrobe (no longer standing)
Well • White (the oldest)

THE HOUSE THAT WASN'T

In Leinster Terrace W2 is a Victorian terrace frontage with windows, a door… and nothing else. It is a beautiful piece of trompe l'oeil measuring 18 inches thick, which was built to disguise a huge air-vent space behind it, part of the Tube network. In a famous hoax of the 1930s, a sharp-eyed conman made himself a quick fortune by selling 10 guinea tickets for a charity ball to be held at the address to hundreds of excited guests, who duly turned up in evening dress and were baffled to get no response when they knocked at the door.

I NAME THIS BOROUGH...

The original meanings of a few London place names

Acton ....*farmstead by the oaks*
Barnet ....*land cleared by burning*
Clerkenwell ....*spring where students gather*
Dulwich ....*marshy meadow where dill grows*
Ealing ....*settlement of Gilla's people*
Fulham ....*Fulla's land in a river bend*
Greenwich ....*green harbour*
Hammersmith ....*place with a hammer smithy*
Islington ....*Gisla's hill*
Kensal Green ....*place by the king's wood*
Lambeth ....*landing place for lambs*
Mayfair ....*the place of the May fair*
      (*held there in seventeenth and eighteenth century*)
Neasden ....*place by the nose-shaped hill*
Osterley ....*woodland clearing with a sheepfold*
Putney ....*landing place where hawks are seen*
Roehampton ....*home farm where rooks are seen*
Spitalfields ....*hospital fields*
Theydon Bois ....*de Bosco's estate in the valley*
      where thatching materials are obtained
Upminster ....*higher church*
Vauxhall ....*Falke's hall or manor*
Walthamstow ....*place where guests are welcome*

IT SPOILS ONE'S VIEW

Until 1954, it was forbidden for a building to be taller than the width of the street that it was on, which some ascribe to the fact that Queen Victoria's view from Buckingham Palace had been obscured by a 14-storey hotel, to her considerable fury. However, the result was that many roads were made wider – hence the vast expanse of roads such as Northumberland Avenue, a short stroll from the Palace.

Long Meg of Westminster was supposedly a formidably tall and bawdy woman whose deeds became the subject of ballads and pamphlets, and were even made into a comic play performed in London in 1595. Described by some as 'a lower-class roaring-girl', she joined in the fashion for cross-dressing, which brought her condemnation down from the king and his churchmen.

In Captain Grose's *Dictionary of the Vulgar Tongue*, Meg's nickname was 'a jeering name for a tall woman', and she is mentioned in another book, *The Sword Through the Centuries*, as having vanquished a Spanish knight with her sword and buckler. However, some historians doubt that she was an actual person, and she may have existed only in folklore. Her name has since been given to several objects of unusual size: the large blue-black marble in the south cloister of Westminster Abbey, over the grave of Gervasius de Blois, is called 'Long Meg of Westminster', and her name also refers to a gun in the Tower of London. And the *Edinburgh Antiquarian Magazine* in September 1769 wrote of a Peter Branan, aged 104, who was 6ft 6in tall and was commonly called Long Meg of Westminster.

We can also only assume that, if she did exist, being called Long Meg rather than Tall Meg had a certain significance.

SMOKING BANS ARE NOT JUST 21ST-CENTURY

The now-defunct Marlborough Club was established by the future Edward VII, when he was sent to the smoking room in White's to enjoy a cigar. In a fit of pique, he set up his own club, where he could smoke whenever he wanted.

LONDON SONGS

'London Calling' – *The Clash*
'The Lambeth Walk' – *Rose, Furber and Gay*
'Maybe It's Because I'm a Londoner' – *Hubert Gregg*
'London Town' – *Buck's Fizz*
'Waterloo Sunset' – *the Kinks*

TUBE TRIVIA

- The shortest Tube line is the Waterloo and City line, which covers just 1.5 miles.
- The longest continuous journey possible is 34 miles, from West Ruislip to Epping on the Central Line.
- The longest distance between stations is four miles between Chesham and Chalfont & Latimer on the Metropolitan line.
- The shortest distance between tube stations is 0.16 miles, the distance between Leicester Square and Covent Garden on the Piccadilly line.
- The District Line has the most stations (60) and Waterloo & City the fewest (2).
- The oldest subway line in the world is the Metropolitan line. It opened on 10 January 1863.
- The peak hour for tube suicides is 11am.
- Around half a million mice live on the Underground. No one has yet counted the rats.
- The Underground has a total of 408 escalators.
- Waterloo Station has the most escalators – 25.
- The deepest station is Hampstead at 58.5m.
- The busiest station is Victoria, which handles up to 100 million passengers a year.
- The longest escalator is at Angel, measuring 60m, rising to 27.5m.
- Gladstone and Dr Barnardo were the only two people to have their coffins transported by Tube.

OLD PICTURE, NEW CAPTION

In its early days, the National Gallery experimented with various ways to encourage visitors to linger longer

A HEARTFELT TALE

Bleeding Heart Yard was named by someone with a taste for the literal, as it was there that a seventeenth century society beauty was found dead after jilting her lover, the Spanish Ambassador. Elizabeth Hatton rejected her suitor in 1626, but was seen dancing with him at a ball not long afterwards. When she left the party, the other guests assumed she was with the Ambassador, but in fact she had been horribly murdered and her body was found outside in the yard the next morning. The case is referred to in Dickens's *Little Dorrit*: 'At dawn the body of Lady Hatton was found in the courtyard behind the stables torn limb from limb with her heart still pumping blood on to the cobblestones.' The site is now occupied by The Bleeding Heart Restaurant, which serves a fine rare steak.

THE NAME OF THE ROAD

The origin of some of London's street names

Bloomsbury Square, WC1
Bloomsbury is named after a Norman nobleman, who was given ownership of the land in this area by William the Conqueror.

Maiden Lane, WC2
Named after middens, which are rubbish heaps.

Cannon Street, EC4
Originally Candle Street, filled with candlemakers.

Cloak Lane, EC4
Open sewer street, as in the Roman's Cloaca Maxima (the Great Drain).

Gloucester Road, SW7
Once called Hogmore Lane, but renamed when the Duchess of Gloucester moved in at the beginning of the nineteenth century.

Seven Sisters Road, N4
Named after the seven daughters of Robert the Bruce, who planted seven elm trees on Seven Sisters Road.

Herne Hill, SE24
Once the home of a heron or herne, as the river Effra ran through here.

Newgate Street, EC1
Built in the second century, this is 'new' only in comparison to the Old Gate (Aldgate).

Pall Mall, SW1
Named after 'paille maille', a French ball and mallet game once played there.

Pudding Lane, EC3
'Pudding' in this case was not the treacle sponge kind but another word for offal.

Scotland Yard, SW1
The original Yard, Great Scotland Yard, was where the king of Scotland would stay when visiting his English counterpart.

Spitalfields
Truncated version of Hospital Fields; a hospital first stood on this site in 1197.

PATRON SAINTS OF LONDON

A few patron saints that might be needed in London

Actors	*St Genesius, St Vitus*
Architects	*St Thomas, St Barbara*
Bankers	*St Matthew*
Beggars	*St Martin of Tours*
Broadcasters	*Angel Gabriel*
Cab drivers	*St Fiacre*
Civil servants	*Thomas More*
Editors	*St John Bosco*
Hoteliers	*St Gentian, St Amand*
Innkeepers	*St Amand, St Martin of Tours, St Gentian*
Journalists	*St Francis of Sales*
Judges	*St John of Capistrano*
Lawyers	*St Genesius, St Ivo, Thomas More*
Lost articles	*St Anthony of Padua*
Messengers	*Angel Gabriel*
Politicians	*Thomas More*
Tax collectors	*St Matthew*

SOUNDS FAMILIAR

The Festival of Britain may ring a few bells with today's London residents. It was held on derelict land near Waterloo. Most of it was held within the Dome of Discovery, surrounded by pavilions dedicated to educational, scientific exhibitions. There was also the Skylon, a cigar-shaped – perhaps gherkin-shaped? – tower. Evelyn Waugh mentioned 'Monstrous constructions appeared on the south bank of the Thames', and Keith Waterhouse harrumphed that the whole thing was 'a monument to British tat; escalators which didn't work, elegant glass entrance halls stuck over with scrawled notices reading "Use other door"...'

SIGNIFICANT STATUES

Marble Arch was designed by John Nash in 1827 to celebrate the victories at Trafalgar and Waterloo and was intended to stand in the grounds of Buckingham Palace, as an entrance arch for the royal residents. But it met with many obstacles: the foundations proved tricky; the friezes intended for its façade were put up on the Palace instead; a statue of George IV that should have sat on top ended up in Trafalgar Square; and the arch was eventually thought to be standing too close to the Palace. So it was moved to its current location, where it is stranded rather sadly on a traffic island at the far end of Oxford Street. But it has had its uses – instead of being solid, as many assume, it contains three small rooms, one at the top and two behind the sculpted panels. During the 1855 Hyde Park riots, the police used it as a hiding place, from where they took the rioters by surprise when they sprang out unexpectedly. The police continued to use it for observation purposes until 1950.

CAPITAL CONUNDRUMS

What's fishy about St John's Wood tube station?
Answer on page 144

TAKE TEN PACES...

St James's Street, London SW1, opens out through onto the historic Pickering Place – not only the smallest public square in Great Britain with original gas lighting, but also the square in which the last duel in Great Britain was fought. A plaque on the wall erected by the Anglo-Texan Society indicates that from 1842–45 a building here was occupied by the Legation from Republic of Texas to the Court of St James's.

THE BIG STINK

Until the nineteenth century, London had no waste disposal system. Waste of all kinds was simply emptied into the many waterways, creating a vast open sewer, which was also a source of drinking water for many of the residents (beer was considered a healthier alternative – even for breakfast). Cholera seized the city from 1848–1849, 1853–1854 and 1865–1866, killing around 30,000 people. As the population grew, the situation became unbearable, particularly in the hot summer of 1858. The temperatures shot up to 35°C, creating a smell so bad that the windows of the Houses of Parliament had to be covered with sheets soaked in lime carbide to try to keep out the stench. The authorities tried to disinfect the source with carbolic acid, but to little effect. This was useful to Joseph Bazalgette, the chief engineer of the Metropolitan Board of Works, who in 1855 had begun to draw up plans for a vast sewerage system that comprised 1240 miles of tunnels. The long-suffering government gladly gave permission for construction to begin, and when the work was done, London had some of the cleanest water in Europe. But it took until 1974 before any fish were brave enough to test the new, cleaner waters.

LAST TO GO

The last beheading to take place at the Tower of London was of Simon Fraser, Lord Lovat in 1747. The last execution was of German spy Josef Jakobs, who faced a firing squad on 15 August 1941. His execution chair is now in a museum in Leeds, but, according to one of the tour guides, before it was moved, his relatives paid a visit and took a snap of his grandchildren sitting in the chair in which he was shot.

FLESH, FISH AND FOWL ROADS

A menagerie of London road names

Albacore Crescent, *SE13*
Badger Court, *NW2*
Camel Road, *E16*
Dog Lane, *NW10*
Elephant Lane, *SE16*
Fish Street Hill, *EC3*
Goat House Bridge, *SE25*
Hare Street, *SE18*
Ibis Lane, *W4*
Jay Mews, *SW7*
Kingfisher Avenue, *E11*
Lamb Street, *E1*
Magpie Close, *NW9*
Nightingale Lane, *SW12*
Oyster Row, *E1*
Pelican Stairs, *E1*
Rabbit Row, *W8*
Sheep Lane, *E8*
Three Colts Lane, *E2*
Wagtail Close, *NW9*

RIOTING IN THE STREETS

On 6 March 1848, 10,000 people massed in Trafalgar Square to protest against the raising of income tax from three per cent to five per cent. The key speaker, a Mr Reynolds, was seized by police after he told the crowd that he would inter the king of France in Woombles Menagerie. At his arrest, the crowd turned on the police, and began to advance on St James's Park, crying 'To the Palace! Bread and revolution!' but were prevented from storming the palace when the police sealed off the route, and the would-be riot was quickly squashed.

LONDON'S THAMES BRIDGES

Name	Type	Date first opened
Queen Elizabeth II	road	1991
Tower	road	1894
London	road	1831
Alexandra	rail	1866
Southwark	road	1819
Millennium	foot	2000 (reopened 2002)
Blackfriars	rail	1864
Blackfriars	road	1769
Waterloo	road	1817
Hungerford	rail and foot	1863
Westminster	road	1750
Lambeth	road	1862
Vauxhall	road	1816
Grosvenor	rail	1860
Chelsea	road	1934
Albert	road	1873
Battersea	road	1772
Battersea	rail	1863
Wandsworth	road	1873
Putney	rail	1889
Putney	road	1729
Hammersmith	road	1827
Barnes	rail and foot	1849
Chiswick	road	1933
Kew	rail	1869
Kew	road	1759
Richmond Lock	foot	1894
Twickenham	road	1933
Richmond	rail	1848
Richmond	road	1777
Teddington Lock	foot	1889
Kingston	road	1828
Hampton Court	road	1753

LONDON MARATHON FACTS

- The first London marathon took place in March 1982
- The race was founded by former Olympic champion Chris Brasher
- The first sponsor was Gillette, who stumped up £50,000
- In 1982, 20,000 people applied to enter the marathon. This rose to 80,500 in 2004
- In 1982, 7,747 were accepted; this was 46,500 in 2004
- 6,255 runners crossed the finish line in 1982, compared to 32,563 in 2004
- Other sponsors have included Mars (1983–88), Nutrasweet (1993–95), Flora (1996–2006)
- In 2004, identical quadruplets Alison, Brooke, Claire and Darcy Hansen all ran the marathon
- Favourite costumes: two men wearing a strap-on plastic Mini Cooper body (2001); a man dressed up as a phone box (2004)
- One of the slowest ever finishing times was set in 2003 by a man in a vintage 130lb diving suit, who took five days, eight hours, 29 minutes and 46 seconds to finish the race
- The London Marathon has raised around £200 million for charity since 1982 and has become a world-renowned race

NOTORIOUS LONDON PUBS

The Bow Tavern

This now demolished pub on St Giles High Street was where condemned prisoners stopped for their last pint of ale on their way from Newgate Prison to Tyburn Gallows (now Marble Arch). If the executioner rode on the same cart, he was not allowed a drink – hence the phrase 'on the wagon'.

SIGNIFICANT STATUES

Eleanor's crosses

When Eleanor of Castile, the queen of Edward I, died suddenly in 1290, she was commemorated by her grieving spouse by a series of 12 gothic stone spires. One spire was placed at each spot where her funeral cortege rested on its journey from Nottinghamshire, where she died, to Westminster Abbey, where she was buried. Only two of the original crosses survive, in Hertfordshire and Northampton. The last of Eleanor's crosses was erected at Charing Cross, but the spire that is there now is a nineteenth-century replacement.

SONGS ABOUT LONDON THAT WERE NEVER MADE (SADLY)

House of the Rising Sunbury
Hatton My Sleeve
Holborn Under A Bad Sign
Norbury Told Me (There'd Be Days Like These)

NOT THAT LONDON

London is the capital of Christmas Island in Polynesia. 'Discovered' on Christmas Day 1643, the island was purchased from the Singapore government by Australia for £2.9 million pounds in 1957 and is now an Australian territory. Population: 433

London is also an industrial city in south-east Ontario, Canada, which bears some parallels to its English namesake. It has its own Victoria Park, Covent Garden Market, St Paul's Cathedral, Blackfriars Bridge and district of Ealing, and the centre was destroyed by fire in 1844 and 1845 and rebuilt. Population: 336,539.

OLD PICTURE, NEW CAPTION

*Arthur spent his Sundays thinking up new
ways to avoid the congestion charge*

MADE IN LONDON

The first **British-built petrol-driven internal combustion
engine car** was built by Frederick Bremer at his home in
Walthamstow, and first took to the road in 1892. The car
can be seen at the Vestry House Museum, E17.

BENEATH THE CITY

Subterranean relics of London's history

Relic	Underneath where?
Norman crypt	*Church of St Bartholomew the Great, Smithfield*
Norman crypt	*Church of St Mary-le-Bow*
Remains of Giltspur Street Compter (debtor's prison)	*Viaduct Tavern, EC4*
Medieval cellars	*The Olde Cheshire Cheese, Fleet Street*
Thirteenth century crypt	*Sequestered St Etheldreda, Ely Place EC1*
Thirteenth century crypt	*Guildhall, EC2*
Eighteenth century Roman style plunge bath	*Strand Lane*
Underground tunnels and cellars plus a cell for shoplifters	*Harrods*
Remains of the Clerkenwell House of Detention	*Clerkenwell*
190 miles of shelving holding 12 million books	*British Library, Euston Road*
Carlo Gatti's ice wells, c.1860	*King's Cross (London Canal Museum)*
Twelfth century crypt	*All Hallows Staining*
Full-sized steam train	*Wembley Stadium (it was part of an abandoned building scheme)*
A never-completed Tube station	*1 Hampstead Way*

I'M PUTTING ON MY TOP HAT

In January 1797, hatter John Etherington caused a public disturbance by wearing a hat of his own design outside his shop on the Strand. The sight of him modelling his tall, cylindrical creation drew such a large crowd that one spectator was accidentally pushed through a shop window and Etherington was arrested. However, the event drew the right kind of attention and the hat caught on, and Etherington's top hat soon became all the rage.

THE TREE OF LIFE

While the government was squandering squillions on the Millennium Dome, the new century was being commemorated in a much simpler and more meaningful way by the planting of a tree. A small sapling was planted in the churchyard of Chelsea Old Church in November 2000 to celebrate the birth of Christ – which seems simple enough, but there the plot thickens. It is a piece of Glastonbury Thorn, the legendary tree of Glastonbury, which is supposed to have grown from the staff of Joseph of Arimathea, who planted it in the ground when he landed in Britain with the Holy Grail. The original tree was cut down in a Puritan raid, but a cutting was kept by a priest and replanted. The Queen is sent a cutting at Christmas each year to decorate her Christmas table. Sadly for Chelsea Old Church, despite much care and attention, the Thorn failed to take root. We can only assume that it fell on stony ground.

CAPITAL CONUNDRUMS

Where is London's smallest police station?
Answer on page 144

FISH FACTS

Billingsgate market, now known for its fish, was originally a general market for corn, coal, iron, wine, salt, pottery and miscellaneous goods as well as fish. In 1699 an Act of Parliament made Billingsgate 'a free and open market for all sorts of fish whatsoever' with the exception of the sale of eels. Eels could be sold only by the Dutch fishermen whose boats were moored in the Thames, a privilege granted because they had helped to feed the people of London during the Great Fire. As the market's popularity increased, a permanent building was required, and in 1850 the first Billingsgate Market building was constructed on Lower Thames Street. It soon proved to be inadequate and was demolished in 1873 to make way for a new building, which opened in 1876 and which still stands in Lower Thames Street. Billingsgate is the UK's largest inland fish market and a favourite of London's restaurant chefs. Around 25,000 tonnes of fish and fish products are sold there each year, giving the market an annual turnover of around £200m.

CAN YOU HEAR ME AT THE BACK?

Famous names who have lectured at Speaker's Corner

Tony Benn, *Labour* MP
Frederick Engels, *co-author of* The Communist Manifesto
Marcus Garvey, *black nationalist leader*
Vladimir Lenin, *Marxist and leader of the
1917 Russian revolution*
Karl Marx, *revolutionary communist and
co-author of* The Communist Manifesto
William Morris, *artist, designer and socialist*
George Orwell, *writer*
Christabel Pankhurst, *suffragette*
Ben Tillet, *socialist*

LONDON ON LOCATION

Films shot in Trafalgar Square

- *101 Dalmatians* (1996): Joely Richardson cycles through the square with her dog
- *Arabesque* (1966): director Stanley Donen used a camera mounted on Nelson's Column
- *The Day the Earth Caught Fire* (1961): a CND rally takes place in Trafalgar Square
- *It Happened Here* (1964): a Nazi rally is held in the Square
- *The Avengers* (1998): Fiona Shaw and Uma Thurman crash their getaway balloon into a road sign as they fly over a snowy Trafalgar Square
- *28 Days Later* (2002): apocalyptic thriller features an eerily deserted Square
- *28 Weeks Later* (2006): the sequel, funnily enough...

THE STREETS ARE PAVED WITH GOLD

The third richest man in the country in 2007 was the Duke of Westminster, who was estimated to be worth £4.63 billion. The Duke, otherwise known as Gerald Cavendish Grosvenor, owns 300 acres of London as well as land in Britain, Europe, Asia and America. In 2003, he was made Knight Companion of the Most Noble Order of the Garter, in the same year that he faced a revolt by his tenants because of high maintenance costs in Eaton Square, from which he had to back down. He also owns an art collection worth around £225 million, which includes a £30 million Van Dyck and a £25 million Stubbs. His enormous wealth is eclipsed only by Roman Abramovich, the Russian businessman and owner of Chelsea football club, and Lakshmi Mittal, the steel magnate. The Queen, who has often topped the list in the past, now sits in 229th position, with a mere £320 million.

The word 'hooligan' first began to appear in London police-court reports in the summer of 1898. It became instantly popular, and the papers were soon using every derivation they could create, including hooliganism, hooliganesque, hooliganic, and the verb to hooligan. One London paper, the *Daily Graphic*, referred in 22 August 1898 to 'the avalanche of brutality which, under the name of "Hooliganism"…has cast such a dire slur on the social records of South London'.

The Oxford English Dictionary says that the origin of the word is unknown. But in 1899, a man named Clarence Rook claimed in his book, *Hooligan Nights*, that the word derived from a Patrick Hooligan, a small-time bouncer and thief, who lived in the Borough on the south side of the river. Hooligan frequented a pub called the Lamb and Flag with his family and followers, and was imprisoned for murdering a policeman. Another writer, Earnest Weekley, said in his *Romance of Words* in 1912: 'The original Hooligans were a spirited Irish family of that name whose proceedings enlivened the drab monotony of life in Southwark about fourteen years ago.'

LONDON FACTS AND FIGURES

London has:

- A population of 7.2 million, the largest city in the UK
- 143 parks and gardens
- 233 nightclubs
- 26 street markets
- 267 tube stations
- Almost 21,000 licensed taxis
- Recorded over 15 million overseas visitors in 2006
- About 300 spoken languages

WRITING ON THE WALL

Graffiti spotted in London

The grave of Karl Marx is just another communist plot
Charing Cross Road

Colin Davis can't tell his brass from his oboe
Royal Festival Hall

Lateral thinking is a con. Honest? Yes, straight up
London School of Economics

THE STORY OF THE GLOBE

Towards the end of the last century, the director Sam Wanamaker made it his personal duty to rebuild the Globe Theatre, which was first built in 1599. As a building, its life had been short; partially burned down in 1613 thanks to a cannon that was misfired from the balcony, it was closed for ever in 1642 by the Puritans.

The new Globe duly opened in 1997, although Wanamaker died before he could see his achievement realised. The rebuilt Globe, which sits about 200 yards from its original site, holds only 1,700 people, partly due to fire regulations and partly because people are rather bigger these days. The new Globe is the first building with a thatched roof to be built in London since the Great Fire of 1666, an exception to the city's building regulations that was allowed only because the thatching reed was covered with fire retardant substance, bedded on fireboards and fitted with discreet sprinklers. Special fire tests on the building materials revealed that the Globe's walls (made of green oak beams and lime plaster) are able to withstand heat of around 1000 degrees for two hours 53 minutes and 37 seconds before actually catching fire.

OLD PICTURE, NEW CAPTION

*When Lucy asked Charles to take her to the
Ritz tea dance, he had no idea what he was
letting himself in for*

IS THAT YOUR BAG?

In 1998, Anthony Noel Kelly was convicted of stealing
body parts from the Royal College of Surgeons, which he
used to make moulds for sculptures at his Shepherd's Bush
studio. The story would have been disturbing enough without the added detail that Neil Lindsay, the embalmer who
helped Kelly to procure the body parts, transported the
human remains to Shepherd's Bush by tube and taxi,
wrapped in black dustbin bags. The crime might have been
overlooked had Kelly not divulged his methods to an arts
journalist in 1996, shortly after which he was arrested.

LONDON LEGENDS

Dick Whittington

Dick Whittington was the son of Sir William Whittington, a Gloucestershire landowner. After his father died in 1358, Dick travelled to London to enrol with the Mercers' Company as an apprentice. Whittington proved to be very astute at trading valuable imported silks and velvets as worn by the court and had become a very rich man by the time he was 40. In 1393 he was made a City alderman, and in 1397 he was appointed by the king to the position of Lord Mayor, as the incumbent had died in office. Whittington was then elected Mayor at the next election, and twice more in his lifetime, effectively making him Lord Mayor four times. He became an important benefactor, creating a library at Greyfriars' Monastery, a refuge for unmarried mothers at St Thomas's Hospital, a large public lavatory and a new church, St Michael Paternoster.

He also made bequests that enabled building work to continue after his death, including the rebuilding of Newgate Gaol, a library at Guildhall, and a college for priests and an almshouse, known as Whittington College, which stood next to St Michael's Church. Although the church burned down in 1666, the college still exists, having moved to Highgate in 1821 and then to West Sussex in 1965, and it is still run with income from the City estate that Whittington left for the purpose. The pantomime fable involving black cats, city bells and affairs with the boss's daughter was first printed in 1605, but the details, except the making of his fortune, are not thought to be true.

LONDON PHRASES

London broil – in the US this is a mixed grill; in the UK it was a boneless cut of beef (as from the shoulder or flank) usually served sliced diagonally across the grain.

Trundling underneath London, Tube passengers sometimes pass through abandoned stations, with dusty platforms and dimly flickering lights. And it might be one of these…

Aldwych: located on the Strand near Surrey Street, it used to run special trains to take theatregoers home. Reroutings meant that the line became little used, and when the lifts needed replacing in 1994 at a cost of £3 million, it was closed.

British Museum: Situated on the north side of High Holborn, this should have interchanged with the line at Holborn, but a proposed subway connection was never built. The new central line at Holborn in 1933 made the station redundant and it was closed.

Brompton Road: Rather too close to South Kensington and Knightsbridge, the station was unpopular, and eventually drivers were ordered to drive through it out of rush hour, which gave rise to the cry 'Passing Brompton Road'. Closed in July 1934.

City Road: Between Old Street and Angel stations, this closed in 1922 while improvements were made, but never reopened. Converted to an air raid shelter in 1941, but abandoned after the war.

Down Street: Opened 1903 between Green Park and Hyde Park Corner, this was too close to both. Closed in 1932.

King William Street: On the corner of King William Street and Arthur Street East, its opening was attended by the Prince of Wales (later Edward VII). Despite many alterations, the badly designed station closed in 1900.

South Kentish Town: Between Camden Town and Kentish Town on the Northern Line, this was closed during a power cut and never reopened.

BIG BEN – THE FACTS

- Big Ben is housed in St Stephen's Tower.
- Big Ben first chimed the hour in July 1859.
- The clock was stopped in 1916, when all public clocks were silenced to prevent them offering directional help to the Germans.
- The chimes of Big Ben were first broadcast on the radio in 1923, and on television in 1949. They are still used in news broadcasts today, and to chime in the New Year.
- In 1944 the clock stopped twice: once when a workmen left a hammer inside and once when a spring broke.
- In 1945 the hammer froze and the clock couldn't strike.
- In 1949 the hands were stopped by swarming starlings.
- The longest stoppage lasted 13 days and took place in 1977 during repairs to the clock.
- The timing of the clock is maintained with old pre-decimalised pennies; adding one to the balance causes the clock to gain two-fifths of a second in 24 hours.
- Big Ben was given a pre-birthday makeover in 2007 in time for its 150th anniversary in 2009.

SIGNIFICANT STATUES

Albert Memorial

When Queen Victoria's beloved husband Prince Albert died of typhoid aged just 41, the queen was so devastated that she went into mourning for many years. She asked Sir George Gilbert Scott to design a fabulous memorial so that Albert would never be forgotten, and Scott came up with a 175 foot overwrought, gothic edifice, with a black and gilded spire, marble canopy, mosaics, enamels, wrought iron and hundreds of sculpted figures. The steps that lead up to the prince are guarded by figures that represent Europe, Africa, America and Asia – thus Victoria had placed the world at her beloved's feet.

In 1348 the Great Plague that had been devastating Europe reached Britain. It was probably not, as was widely believed, bubonic plague, and was not referred to at the time as the Black Death, a phrase that was invented later. But it was still terrifying.

The worst of the deaths were concentrated into three or four months, but the disease continued to flourish until well into 1350. The Plague took rich and poor alike; the rich tried to flee the city, but only took the disease with them. It is estimated that around 20,000 Londoners were killed by the Plague, around a third of the population. Worse still, plague would return to London at regular intervals for centuries to come.

The Great Plague of 1665 was the worst outbreak of this feared disease. The hot summer of 1665 together with the city's increasingly over-crowded population created ideal conditions for the spread of an infectious disease. The poor were not allowed to leave the filthy slums and some tried to isolate themselves by living on boats on the Thames.

Dogs and cats were killed as they were thought to transmit the disease. If a person fell ill, the whole family would be locked into their house for 40 days. Plague doctors and nurses were not qualified and and usually did little more than sell food to the quarantined families. The death toll was breathtaking: thousands died every week, reaching a peak of 7,165 in one week in September. Bodies were buried in mass graves. Historians believe that some 100,000 people died in London during this last Great Plague.

In view of this, The Great Fire of 1666 was almost a blessing – the fire killed only six people, but destroyed large parts of the city and practically all its slums, which at last led to the end of the plague epidemic in London.

SONGS ABOUT LONDON THAT WERE NEVER MADE (SADLY)

Running Up Gants Hill
These Boots Were Made For Wapping
Twenty Four Hours from Tulse Hill
You've Lost That Loving Ealing

RIOTING IN THE STREETS

In 1780, MP Lord George Gordon, the President of the Protestant Association, incited a huge and angry crowd to protest against the dilution of anti-Catholic laws, which until that point had prevented Catholics from owning property, inheriting land and other essential functions. Amid rumours that tens of thousands of Jesuits were concealed in tunnels underneath London, ready to storm the city at any moment, a mob of around 30,000 – some accounts place the total at nearer 50,000 – began rioting on Friday 2 June 1780 with attacks on Catholic places of worship, including the Sardinian Chapel in WC1 and the Bavarian Chapel on Warwick Street. The riots flared over the weekend and continued on until the Tuesday, when Newgate and Clink prisons were attacked and set on fire. The rioters attacked Catholic churches and buildings, as well as judges and other dignitaries, and a group of French protestants (by mistake). The riots were said to be the most violent in London's history. In the end, the militia was called in to restore order, 285 rioters were killed and 450 more imprisoned. Twenty-five were later hanged, although the original troublemaker, Lord George Gordon, surrendered and was cleared of treason. He was later sent to Newgate Prison, once it had been rebuilt, for libelling Marie Antoinette, and he died within its walls.

MR PARROT AND THE
FOUR-MINUTE DASH

While most people think that Roger Bannister ran the first four-minute mile in Oxford in 1954, an historian called Peter Radford thinks differently. He claimed, in 2004, that the record was broken 184 years earlier in London. According to Radford's research, in 1770, a market trader named James Parrot ran a mile from Charterhouse Wall in Goswell Road and then the length of Old Street in under four minutes, to settle a bet – the equivalent of £1,380 in today's money. Radford's theory has upset the scientists, who claim that human athletic abilities improve over the centuries, and that no one could have run that fast in the eighteenth century, especially without the benefit of modern training techniques. But perhaps they overlook the motivational effects of a large pile of cash at the finishing post.

CAPITAL CONUNDRUMS

Where is the centre of London?
Answer on page 144

LONDON FIRSTS

• Alexander Waugh, brother of Evelyn, claimed to have held the first cocktail party in Britain in 1924. Only one guest turned up.
• In 1880 the Telephone Company Ltd issued the first known phone directory. It listed 250 names connected to three London exchanges.
• In 1829 the UK's first scheduled bus service ran between Bank and Marylebone Road. The bus was horse-drawn.
• The UK's first policewomen were Mary Allen and Margaret Dawson, who trod their beat in London in 1914.

In 1780, a builder discovered to his surprise a series of underground caverns in Blackheath, which had been excavated from chalk and were connected by passages, descending to a depth of 160 feet. The caverns were named 'Jack Cade's Caverns' after the rebel leader who had amassed a civil army on Blackheath in 1450, although it is not suggested that he constructed or used them. One theory is that the caverns dated back to the fifth century, when they were used by frightened locals to hide from the invading Saxons and Danes after the withdrawal of the Romans. The other is that they were created when chalk was excavated to help with the construction of St Paul's Cathedral.

When they were rediscovered in 1780, steps were built to lead down into them, and they became first a local point of interest, and, in the nineteenth century, a popular venue for night-time entertainment.

The public could take a torchlight tour of the caves for 4d or 6d; and when a bar, chandelier and ventilation system were installed, drinking parties and balls were held there, the only disadvantage being that if the lights went out (as they often did), panic tended to spoil the party. They were eventually sealed up in 1854. The local council attempted to reopen them in 1906 without success, but they tried again in 1938, with the intention of turning them into air-raid shelters. Graffiti and other mementos of its former life were found, including the brass ring that had held the chandelier, and the council created new ventilation shafts and extra support; however, the caves were never used as shelters as they were not considered safe. Indeed, subsidence has proved a problem; in the worst incident in Kidbrooke in 1798, a hole so large opened up that it swallowed up a horse.

RIOTING IN THE STREETS

On 22 September 1831, the House of Commons introduced the Reform Bill in an attempt to abolish 'rotten boroughs', parliamentary constituencies that had very few voters but still had the power to elect members to the House of Commons. This meant that candidates could easily bribe or cheat their way into power. The Tories were also set against increasing the number of people who were entitled to vote. The House of Commons passed the Reform Bill, but it was defeated by the Tory-dominated House of Lords. When the news broke, there were riots in several British towns, including in London, where the houses owned by the Duke of Wellington and bishops who had voted against the Bill in the Lords were attacked. Finally, on 13 April 1832, the Reform Act was passed by a small majority in the House of Lords.

LONDON ON LOCATION

Some classic London films

The Lodger (1927) • *The Man Who Knew Too Much* (1934) • *Sabotage* (1936) • *Stagefright* (1950) *Oliver Twist* (1948) • *The Blue Lamp* (1949) *Passport to Pimlico* (1949) • *The Ladykillers* (1955) *The Pumpkin Eater* (1964) • *Mary Poppins* (1964) *Blow-Up* (1966) • *Alfie* (1966) • *Georgy Girl* (1966) *To Sir with Love* (1966) • *Performance* (1969) *A Clockwork Orange* (1971) • *Frenzy* (1972) *The Long Good Friday* (1979) • *An American Werewolf in London* (1981) • *Dance with a Stranger* (1984) • *Mona Lisa* (1985) • *My Beautiful Laundrette* (1985) • *Absolute Beginners* (1986) • *Withnail and I* (1987) *A Fish Called Wanda* (1988) • *The Madness of King George* (1994) • *Shakespeare in Love* (1998) *Lock, Stock and Two Smoking Barrels* (1998)

PUB QUIZ

Did you know...

The Mayflower, Rotherhithe Street SE16, is the only pub in England licensed to sell US and UK postage stamps.

Nell of Old Drury, 29 Catherine Street WC2, was once linked to the Theatre Royal, and had an intermission bell in the pub to alert drinkers to the second half, and a tunnel once linked the theatre to the pub.

Two Brewers, 40 Monmouth Street WC2, was once called the Sheep's Head, as the severed head of a sheep was put outside the pub every day.

Lamb and Flag, Rose Street WC2, was once known as the Bucket of Blood because of fistfights held in the upstairs room.

The Brink's-Mat gold robbery was planned in the **Calthorpe Arms,** Gray's Inn Road. The first policeman to be killed in London was also killed here.

Chequers, Duke Street SW1, was the first pub to be built after the Great Fire of London.

The Old Red Lion, Holborn WC1, once housed Oliver Cromwell's headless body.

Copies of *The Times* cover the walls of **The Thunderer,** Mount Pleasant Street WC1, as the paper was once called 'The Thunderer'.

Seven Stars, Carey Street WC2, an early seventeenth century pub is one of the smallest in London.

MADE IN LONDON

John Logie Baird first demonstrated the **television** in January 1926 at 22 Frith Street W1.

STRANGER THAN FICTION

When St Paul's Cathedral burned down in 1666, the only monument left standing on the site was that of the poet John Donne – who had also been Dean of St Paul's for the last 10 years of his life.

LENIN WAS HERE

Russian revolutionary Lenin took refuge in London in the early 1900s, finding safety at the following addresses:

22 Ampton Street: where the 2nd Congress of the Russian Social-Democratic Labour Party was held
British Library Reading Room: where he signed in as Jacob Richter and worked at seat L13
14 Frederick Street: his London mailing address
26 Granville Square: where the editorial board of the revolutionary newspaper *Iskra* met
30 Holford Square: his first London address, where he and his wife posed as the Jacob Richters
16 Percy Circus: his home on his second visit to London in 1905, to attend the 3rd Congress of the Russian Social-Democratic Labour Party
20 Regent Square: used by *Iskra* as a mailing address
36 Tavistock Place: lived here in 1908 to carry out research at the British Library
37A Clerkenwell Place: Lenin worked on *Iskra* at the Twentieth Century Press at this address until April 1903.

NOTORIOUS LONDON PUBS

The Magdala, Hampstead

Ruth Ellis shot her lover, David Blakely, outside this pub in 1955 and, when convicted, became the last woman to be hanged in England.

OLD PICTURE, NEW CAPTION

Carruthers demonstrated the strength of his feelings about the pigeons in Trafalgar Square

MIXED SIGNALS

Until 1750 there were only two ways to cross the Thames, over London Bridge or on the horse-ferry between Lambeth and Millbank. However there were plenty of enterprising boatmen willing to row you across for a small fee. They would row up and down the Thames, calling out 'Oars! Oars!' to passers-by, which worked perfectly well with London residents. However, visitors were inclined to mistake this offer for something less savoury, as they assumed that the boatmen were dropping their aitches.

LIGHT FANTASTIC

Who turned on the Oxford Street Christmas lights?

1981	Miss World
1982	Daley Thompson
1983	Pat Phoenix
1984	Esther Rantzen
1985	Bob Geldof
1986	Den and Angie Watts (Leslie Grantham and Anita Dobson)
1987	Derek Jameson
1988	Terry Wogan
1989	Gordon Kay
1990	Cliff Richard
1991	Children from the Westminster Children's Hospital
1992	Linford Christie
1993	Richard Branson
1994	Lenny Henry
1995	The cast of Coronation Street
1996	The Spice Girls
1997	Peter Andre
1998	Zoe Ball
1999	Ronan Keating
2000	Charlotte Church
2001	S Club 7
2002	Blue
2003	Enrique Iglesias
2004	Emma Watson
2005	Westlife
2006	All Saints

CAPITAL CONUNDRUMS

Where is the Chicken Run?
Answer on page 144

PROBLEM PENSIONERS

In *Brewer's Rogues, Villains and Eccentrics*, William Donaldson relates the sorry tale of pensioner Sid Chaney who in 1994 opened an account at Barclays Bank in Camden Town in the name of his ferret, improbably called Sir Andrew Large. Chaney then opened another account at the City branch of the NatWest Bank in N1 in the name of Mr Sniffles, his cat, and another in the name of his budgerigar, Captain Mainwaring. Easily escaping the attentions of the banks' security procedures, in no time at all he and his pets ran up a debt of £117,000. On the one occasion when a vetting procedure would have been appropriate, it was conspicuous by its absence. Mr Chaney escaped prosecution except by American Express, whose debt of £11,500 he is paying off at £1 a week, which should take him 230 years.

TUNNEL VISION

In October 1940 the government agreed to build eight deep-level shelters, which was eventually increased to 10, at Clapham South, Clapham Common, Clapham North, Stockwell, Oval, St Paul's, Chancery Lane, Goodge Street, Camden Town and Belsize Park. They would be built 85-105 feet deep, and access would be by a shaft sunk at either end of the tunnel, with staircases separate to the existing ones, emerging in above-level block houses made from reinforced concrete.

Not all of the proposed stations were built – Oval and St Paul's were abandoned – but the block-houses for the remaining shelters can still be seen. After the war it was suggested that the deep tunnels be used to create an express Northern line service, running non-stop into the West End. Sadly, as Northern Line regulars can attest, this idea was never developed.

The City Wall was first constructed by the Romans around AD 200. It took about 10 years to build and ran between two landmarks that were not there when the wall was built, but are now the Tower of London and Blackfriars railway station. It was nearly two miles in length, and enclosed an area of 330 acres. It was between six and nine feet wide and about 18 feet high and incorporated the north and west side of an existing 12-acre Roman fort, and would take about an hour to walk its length. There were large city gates at strategic points along the wall to allow traffic in and out of the City, remnants of which can be seen in the names Ludgate, Newgate, Aldersgate, Cripple-gate, Bishopsgate and Aldgate.

A series of towers were added in the thirteenth century, and a ditch dug around the outside to improve defences. Two of the 20 towers survive: one at the Barbican, and one that has been incorporated into the Barber-Surgeons Hall. The towers were home to hermits in peacetime. The limits of the city remained largely unchanged until the wall was thought no longer necessary for defence in the 1700s, and the ditch had become a nuisance, as it was used as a rubbish dump. Most of the wall was demolished in 1760, and any parts that could not easily be torn down were incorporated into shops. The wall explains that strange name of 'St Botolph's without Aldersgate'; St Botolph's was outside, or without, the city wall. He was the patron saint of travellers, so people would ask for his blessing as they left the city walls. There were originally four St Botolph churches for this purpose, although one was destroyed in the Great Fire of London. A few remnants remain within the walls of the Museum of London, and there is another outside Tower Hill tube station.

LONGEST-SERVING
COMMITTEE MEMBER

Jeremy Bentham was an eighteenth-century philosopher whose macabre sense of humour has left London with a peculiar legacy. He left a large sum of money to University College on condition that when he died, his skeleton would continue to attend the annual general meeting. His skeleton is duly wheeled along to the AGM each year, preserved in a mahogany case, seated in a chair and holding his favourite walking stick. Bentham is also taken to the weekly meeting of the board of governors, where he is recorded as present but is not allowed to vote.

MODERN TALES OF LONDON

City of Spades, Colin McCabe (1957)
Mr Love and Justice, Colin McCabe (1960)
Sour Sweet, Timothy Mo (1982)
Money, Martin Amis (1984)
London Fields, Martin Amis (1989)
The Buddha of Suburbia, Hanif Kureishi (1990)
Fever Pitch, Nick Hornby (1992)
Hawksmoor, Peter Ackroyd (1993)
Downriver, Iain Sinclair (1995)
While England Sleeps, David Leavitt (1995)
Grey Area, Will Self (1996)
High Fidelity, Nick Hornby (1996)
Lights Out for the Territory, Iain Sinclair (1997)
Metroland, Julian Barnes (1997)
Armadillo, William Boyd (1998)
Capital, Maureen Duffy (2001)
White Teeth, Zadie Smith (2001)
The Bat Tattoo, Russell Hoban (2002)
Fingersmith, Sarah Waters (2002)
Brick Lane, Monica Ali (2004)

COCKNEY LONDON

A few London place names and their Cockney meanings

Boat Race	*face*
Chalk Farm	*arm*
Conan Doyle	*boil*
Daily Mail	*tale*
Doctor Crippen	*dripping*
Duke of York	*balk, cork or fork*
Hampstead Heath	*teeth*
Harvey Nichols	*pickles*
Jack the Ripper	*kipper*
Lord Mayor	*swear*
Newington Butts	*guts*
Richard the Third	*bird*

FERRY STRANGE

Before the Thames had bridges, William Overs was one of the many ferrymen who would row you across to the other side. Mr Overs was so mean that in order to save on housekeeping, he faked his own death, as mourning usually meant a day or two of fasting. But Overs overestimated his family's affections, as, on hearing of his demise, they threw a party instead. To punish them, he sat up suddenly in the middle of the party, where his body had been laid out for all to see, but one guest, thinking he had risen from the dead, took one of Overs's oars and hit him over the head with it, killing him instantly. Meanwhile, Overs's daughter Mary had sent for her boyfriend – barred from the house by her father – who rode his horse at such speed to join his lover that he fell off and died. Distraught, Mary used the profits of the ferry business to found a convent, to which was attached the Church of St Mary Overie, now known as Southwark Cathedral.

LONDON LEGENDS

Ronnie Scott

While jazz musician Ronnie Scott will be remembered for his legendary jazz club in Soho, he should also be remembered for his self-deprecation and refusal to take life too seriously. In his obituary in the *Daily Telegraph*, Scott was fondly remembered by the writer for his truly terrible jokes, in which he often insulted his audience for being somewhat inert in their response. While he claimed to have opened his club to guarantee that he would have somewhere to play, he was an accomplished musician and played with many of the greats, as well as recording several albums, including one called 'Never Pat a Burning Dog'. His club moved to its current address in Frith Street in 1965, and offered jazz six nights a week, which was radical for Britain at the time. His club played host to the likes of Count Basie and Ella Fitzgerald; The Who held the premiere of *Tommy* there, and Jimi Hendrix gave his last performance there before his untimely death. The club's fortunes declined until it was bought by Chris Blackwell of Island Records, who donated £25,000 on the understanding that absolutely nothing was to be changed. It was further saved by a jazz revival in the 80s. Scott played sax on the Beatles' 'Lady Madonna'. The title of Ronnie's 1989 biography had the last laugh by immortalising his attitude to his customers: *Let's All Join Hands and Contact the Living*.

A NICE SPOT FOR A PICNIC

On 23 October 1843, 14 people ate a meal on the platform at the top of Nelson's Column, just before the statue of Nelson was erected.

Sir Charles Barry (1795–1860): Houses of Parliament, Travellers Club in Pall Mall, Reform Club

Edward Middleton Barry (1830–1880): completed his father's work on the Houses of Parliament

Sir William Chambers (1723–1796): Kew Gardens pagoda, Somerset House (1776)

Norman, Lord Foster (1935–): British Museum Great Court, HSBC HQ at Canary Wharf, No.1 London Wall, Tower Place, Canary Wharf station, Sir Alexander Fleming Building at Imperial College, Swiss Re HQ ('The Gherkin'), Millennium Bridge, City Hall

James Gibbs (1682–1754): St Martin-in-the-Fields (1726)

Nicholas Hawksmoor (1661–1736): St George's Church in Bloomsbury, Christ Church in Spitalfields.

Sir Denys Louis Lasdun (1914– 2001): Royal College of Physicians, National Theatre, Hallfield Estate, Keeling House

Sir Edwin Landseer Lutyens (1869–1944): Cenotaph, Whitehall, the Grosvenor Estate

John Nash (1752–1835): Marble Arch, Regent Street, recreated Buckingham Palace from Buckingham House

Sir Joseph Paxton (1801–1865): Great Exhibition Building of 1851, Crystal Palace

Sir John Soane (1753–1837): Bank of England, Dulwich Picture Gallery, Sir John Soane Museum

Inigo Jones (1573–1652):
Queen's House at Greenwich; rebuilt the Banqueting Hall, parts of old St Paul's (before 1666), the Queen's Chapel at Marlborough House

Sir Robert Smirke (1781–1867):
Covent Garden Theatre, British Museum, King's College, Royal College of Physicians

Lord Richard Rogers (1933–):
Lloyd's Building, Millennium Dome

Sir George Gilbert Scott (1811–1878):
Albert Memorial, St Pancras

Norman Shaw (1831–1912):
Old Swan House, Chelsea, New Scotland Yard, Gaiety Theatre, Aldwych, Piccadilly Hotel

Sir John Wolfe-Barry (1836–1918):
Tower Bridge

Sir Christopher Wren (1632–1723):
51 London churches, including St Paul's (rebuilt after 1666), Chelsea Hospital, Greenwich Observatory, parts of Hampton Court Palace and the Royal Naval College, St Clement Dane in the Strand, St James in Piccadilly, St Mary le Bow, Cheapside.

HARSH BUT FAIR?

At midnight on 19 June 1810, a labourer named Thomas Hart of the parish of Saint Mary Stratford Bow broke into the house of James Lindsay and stole a shirt worth three shillings. He was found guilty – and sentenced to seven years' transportation. He had reason to be grateful for this sentence. Had it been the sixteenth century, he could have been hanged, which was the penalty for the theft of any goods worth more than a shilling. Instead he spent seven years in Australia – though it is not known if the courts gave him a return ticket for when his sentence was up.

OLD PICTURE, NEW CAPTION

*When the 8.32 to Clapham Junction
became unreasonably overcrowded, Jeremy
took matters into his own hands.*

SPORTING LONDON

In London in July 1985, Boris Becker became the youngest
man ever to win Wimbledon, when at the age of 17 years
and 7 months he beat the unseeded Kevin Curran in four
sets: 6-3, 6-7, 7-6, 6-4. He was also the first German and
the first unseeded player to win the tournament. To dismiss
claims of a fluke, he beat Ivan Lendl the following year
to take the title again, and reached the finals in the following three years, winning for the third and last time in
1989 by beating Stefan Edberg in three sets. Edberg got
his own back the following year, when the pair faced
each other in the finals once more, and Edberg beat Becker
in five gruelling sets. In all, Becker reached the Wimbledon
finals seven times in 10 years.

RIOTING IN THE STREETS

In June 1450, Jack Cade led tens of thousands of rebellious peasants to London to protest at the incompetence of King Henry VI and his government, unfair taxes, corruption and the recent loss of France. Alarmed, Henry fled to Warwickshire, leaving the city to its fate. The rebels took possession of Southwark, executed the Lord Treasurer and others, and, against Jack Cade's instructions, looted, robbed and raped at will. Captain Matthew Gough led a group of men to defeat the rioters, and a fierce battle was fought back and forth across London Bridge. Captain Gough was killed, and the Lord Treasurer, Archbishop John Kemp, called for a truce; the rebels chose to leave with their plunder and a pardon, but Cade was soon hunted down and taken prisoner. He died on the way back to London, after which dozens more rebels were executed.

SPIRITS IN THE SKY

In 1829, Thomas Willson had an idea that he thought would solve London's chronically congested graveyards; build a burial pyramid. His plans showed a construction that would stand taller than today's Canary Wharf and would hold five million dead bodies. The burial sites on each of his pyramid's 94 floors would be reached by steam-powered lifts. His scheme was not taken up by the government, who opted for the more British way of burying their dead – underground and out of sight.

WHO NAMED THE THAMES?

No name is recorded for London's main river before Julius Caesar referred to it as Tamesis. After 'Kent', this is the oldest place name in England.

NOTORIOUS LONDON PUBS

Blind Beggar, Whitechapel Road

Where Ronnie Kray's murdered one of his many
enemies, George Cornell, by shooting him through
the eye. By strange coincidence, given the pub's name,
this was also where Bulldog Wallis, a pickpocket
and ruffian, killed a man by pushing an umbrella
tip through his eye.

GOING UNDERGROUND

The map of the London Underground, one of the capital's most recognisable icons, was created by a 28-year-old draughtsman called Henry Beck, who in 1931 was laid off from his job. Short of things to do, he fell to thinking about the Tube map and how it might be improved; at the time it was based on a street map, and was geographically more accurate than the current version. Beck redrew it with three principles in mind: that it should be a diagram rather than a map; that the centre should be enlarged in proportion to the outskirts for greater clarity; and that every line should be either vertical, horizontal or a 45-degree diagonal. The resulting map was clear, simple to understand and a work of graphic genius. Needless to say, his superiors disagreed at first, but fortunately he persuaded them to print 500 copies as a trial. It was an instant success, and by 1933 had completely replaced its predecessor. Beck continued to refine his map, although it took him 16 years to hit on the idea of using a white circle and connecting line to show where stations interchanged. The final edition of Beck's iconic map was printed in 1959, after which time his name was removed and the map is now copyrighted to London Regional Transport. But his work will never be forgotten.

BRING IN THE FLYING SQUAD

Robberies and attempted robberies at Heathrow airport

November 1983	Gold bars and diamonds worth £26 million stolen. The thieves were apprehended and jailed for 25 years
December 1991	Police prevent an attempt to kidnap an airline worker in order to gain access to a warehouse containing £26 million worth of goods
August 1994	£850,000 in used banknotes stolen by thieves who used tear gas to overcome the unfortunate courier
January 2000	A man hid in the hold of flight to Madrid in order to steal £1.5 million in Spanish currency. He was arrested on the return flight
February 2002	£4.57 million in foreign currency stolen from a BA security van
February 2002	26,000 mobile phones stolen from a Samsung warehouse
March 2002	Police arrest 12 people attempting to hijack a van carrying £1.8 million
May 2004	100 police overpower eight armed robbers attempting to steal £40 million in gold bullion and £40 million in cash from a warehouse

LONG TALL ALLEY

London's narrowest alleyway Brydges Place, which connects Bedfordbury in Covent Garden to St Martin's Lane. Two hundred yards long, it is, at its narrowest point, only 15 inches wide. It is dark, dank and faintly odorous. For the mischievous, it is also a good place to dart out unexpectedly and alarm innocent tourists.

EXTREME STATISTICS

- London has the highest population of any European city.
- London has the busiest airport in Europe: Heathrow handles over 60 million passengers a year.
- London has the most congested ring-road in Europe, the M25
- Oxford Street is the busiest shopping street in Europe, with 200 million visitors a year and a total turnover of £5 billion.
- London has the most street markets of any city in the western world.
- There are more billionaires in London than there are in any other world city.
- London was the first city in the world after the Middle Ages where the population exceeded 1 million. In 1811, there were 1,009,546 people in the city. It remained the largest city in the world until 1957, when it was overtaken by Tokyo.
- London has the sixth largest library in the world, which is the British Library. It was founded in 1753 and contains 15 million books.
- London has the largest local authority archives in the entire United Kingdom.
- London holds the oldest dedicated collection of clocks and watches in the world, at the Guildhall Library.
- London has the longest escalator in western Europe at Angel Underground Station, which consists of 318 steps.
- London has the longest underground rail network in the world, which comprises a total length of 392 kilometres of track.
- London has the fourth longest underground tunnel in the world, the Northern Line from East Finchley to Morden. It was completed in 1939 and measures 27.8 kilometres in length.

LET ME TAKE YOU UNDER
THE STREETS OF LONDON

In December 1980, journalist Duncan Campbell took an unusual walk from East London to Westminster – underground. In a report for the *New Statesman*, he climbed (illegally) down an access shaft in Bethnal Green Road 100 feet below the surface to a well-lit tunnel and started to cycle to Westmister. He found an extraordinary and extensive network of well-maintained tunnels below the city . His route at first converged with the Central line tube tunnel, the Mail Rail tunnel (exclusively used by the Post Office) and another tunnel that led to an underground telephone exchange near St Paul's. Campbell didn't need a map, as there were frequent signposts to places of interest such as Whitehall, The Mall and Lord's Cricket Ground.

The tunnels led to Holborn, Covent Garden, Fleet Street, Leicester Square, the Post Office Tower, Waterloo and, of course, Whitehall. Campbell found another telephone exchange just south of Nelson's Column, from where he could have reached (by lift) the Ministry of Defence, the Treasury, the Admiralty and Downing Street. Campbell finally emerged back in the Holborn Telephone Exchange, near to the *New Statesman*'s offices. There are also rumoured to be tunnels from Buckingham Palace to Parliament and Wellington Barracks, whose presence is hinted at by a mysterious extractor fan outside the ICA on the Mall, as well as a set of steps that can be seen by peering through a louvred window in the ICA gents' toilets.

CAPITAL CONUNDRUMS

Who is Great Tom, and what links him with Big Ben?
Answer on page 144

DESIGNING WOMEN

A list of patented inventions exhibited by London women at an exhibition in Chicago in 1883

Portable household washing copper: *Miss Mary Brown, Clapham*

Music folio and stand: *Mrs Bewicke Calverley, St James's Park*

Appliance for lifting hot plates: *Mrs F Tenison, Uxbridge Road*

Clothes washer: *Mrs S Mackie, Chancery Lane*

Sanitary sink basket: *Miss I Peckover, Bloomsbury*

Knee music stand: *Miss M Stephenson*

Specimen of painting on textiles: *Miss D Turck, St George's Square*

Improved ear trumpet: *Mrs M Phillipps, Kilburn*

However, none of the women were quite so ingenious as another member of their group, a Miss Barron from East Moseley, who invented a collapsible noiseless coal-scuttle as well as a combined dress-stand and fire escape made of basketwork.

IMPRESSIONS OF LONDON

Famous paintings of the capital

Lucian Freud ....*Factory in North London*, 1972
Joseph Mallord William Turner................*London*, 1809
James McNeill Whistler ....*London Bridge*, 1885
James McNeill Whistler........*Nocturne in Blue and Gold: Old Battersea Bridge*, 1872-1875
Hans Holbein the Younger.........*Georg Gisze, a German, merchant in London*, 1532
Camille Pissarro ....*Hyde Park, London*, 1890
Camille Pissarro .....*Charing Cross Bridge, London*, 1890
James Tissot................................*London Visitors*, c.1874

IDENTITY CRISIS

When the station we now know as Embankment was opened in May 1870, serving the District Line, it was given the name of Charing Cross. When the Bakerloo line platforms opened there on 10 March 1906, the station was renamed Embankment.

Meanwhile, the station now known as Charing Cross – which also opened to serve the Bakerloo line on 10 March 1906 – was called Trafalgar Square, but was renamed Charing Cross when the Northern Line platforms opened there in June 1907. When the Northern Line platforms also opened at Embankment on 6 April 1914, that station's name was changed again to Charing Cross (Embankment). On the same day, Charing Cross station became Charing Cross (Strand). A year later, on 9 May 1915, both names changed again: Charing Cross (Strand) became Strand and Charing Cross (Embankment) was renamed Charing Cross.

Strand was closed for rebuilding in June 1973; while it was closed, Embankment was renamed Charing Cross Embankment. When Strand reopened on 1 May 1979, now serving the Bakerloo, Northern and Jubilee lines, it was renamed Charing Cross. And finally, on 12 September 1976, Charing Cross Embankment was renamed, simply, Embankment.

And that, we hope, is the end of that.

LONDON SONGS

'London's Burning' – *traditional nursery rhyme*
'Foggy Day in London Town' – *Ira and George Gershwin*
'A Nightingale Sang in Berkeley Square'
– *Maschwitz and Sherwin*
'Waterloo' – *Abba*

COLONEL THOMAS BLOOD

The seventeenth century courtier Colonel Blood was the satisfyingly named thief who attempted to steal the crown jewels in 1671. Colonel Blood took a group of friends to the Tower of London, pulled out a mallet and knocked out the guard guarding the royal treasures. They seized all the treasures except the sceptre, which Blood's companions tried to cut in half to make it easier to hide, but when it proved too tough to cut, they made do with the orb and crown. However, they were arrested at the main gate. Found guilty, Blood faced torture and death; yet Charles II pardoned him and gave him a position at court and later a title and land in Ireland. The popular theory was that Charles had arranged the burglary himself, as a way of raising a bit of cash. However, it seems he might have got away with it after all; when the king died in 1687, it was found that many of the precious stones in the crown jewels had been replaced with cheap copies.

DEADLY VERSE

Ring-a-ring o' roses
A pocket full of posies,
A-tishoo! A-tishoo!
We all fall down.

The nursery rhyme of Ring-a-Ring o' Roses is more of a death knell than a happy verse. It commemorates, in charming euphemisms, the Great Plague of London, which broke out in 1664. The ring of roses is the circular rash that was one of the symptoms; the pocket full of posies refers to the bunches of herbs that people carried to ward off the germs; and the sneezing is the fatal sneeze which many victims suffered just before their final and fatal collapse.

LONDON CLOCKS

Some of London's more interesting clocks, past and present

The Westminster Clock Tower, otherwise fondly known as Big Ben, which is the name of the 13.5 tonne bell that strikes the hour and each quarter.

The mechanical clock at the church of St Dunstan-in-the-West, which overhangs the pavement and has its bell struck on the hour by two apparently indolent giants.

The Apostle Clock, Horniman Museum, which has its own tower.

The Fortnum & Mason clock, which rings the hour and the quarters attracting crowds of tourists.

The Act of Parliament Clock in the George Inn in Borough High Street.

The huge fob watch outside Arthur Saunders watchmaker in Southampton Row.

The Astronomical Clock at Hampton Court Palace, made in 1540.

The Zodiacal Clock over the door of Bracken House, Cannon Street, which also bears the signs of the zodiac and Winston Churchill's scowling face at the centre.

The clock on the tower of the church of St George the Martyr on Borough High Sreet. Of its four faces, the one that faces towards Bermondsey is never illuminated, allegedly because in the past, the people of that parish failed to make donations to the church.

The clock outside the World's End boutique in Chelsea. It runs backwards at speed and has 13 hours.

Sadly no longer to be seen... at the Eccentrics Club on Ryder Street, a clock that ran backwards.

LONDON LEGENDS

William Caxton

William Caxton (*c.*1422 –*c.*1491) was the founder of British printing. Born in Kent, he was a textile merchant's apprentice in London, but upon the death of his master he moved to Bruges and opened his own textile business. He became the governor of the Merchant Adventurers, which meant that he travelled extensively and spoke both Dutch and French. Caxton became an accomplished translator and went to Cologne to study the printing technique developed by Gutenberg. When he returned to London in 1476, Caxton opened his own printing press in Westminster. It is thought that *Dictes or Sayengis of the Philosophres* was the first book that he printed on this press, which was published on 18 November 1477, the first book published in Britain. Caxton published about 100 works, not least Geoffrey Chaucer's *Troilus and Criseyde* and *The Canterbury Tales*. One of these first editions of *The Canterbury Tales* was sold for £4.6 million in 1998. When Caxton died, his assistant, Wynandus van Woerden, better known as Wynkyn de Worde, continued the business, and eventually set up his own printing press in 1500 on Shoe Lane near Fleet Street, thus establishing the centuries-long tradition for that area of the capital as the heart of the British newspaper industry.

LONDON PHRASES

London Rules – boxing rules introduced in 1838 to prevent unfair play such as gouging and headbutting during bare-knuckle fighting; however, they were largely ignored, and London rules is usually meant as a euphemism for 'no rules'.

OLD PICTURE, NEW CAPTION

*Back in the late 19th century, the Regent's
Park Slow Motion Players had great success
with their version of* The Matrix.

SPORTING LONDON

In 2002, the existing world record for the fastest female
marathon runner was broken at the London Marathon
by the UK's Paula Radcliffe, who ran the course in two
hours, 15 minutes and 25 seconds. The world record had
been broken in London twice before: in 1983, Greta
Waitz of Norway clocked up two hours, 25 minutes and
29 seconds, and in 1985 Ingrid Christensen-Kristiansen
of Norway completed the run in two hours, 21 minutes
and six seconds. The world record time for men over the
distance is two hours, four minutes and 26 seconds, set
in the Berlin Marathon, rather than the London one
unfortunately, by Haile Gebrselassie of Ethiopia on
September 30, 2007. All eyes (and feet) are on the
next London marathon in 2008.

HERE BE CRIMINALS

In 1903, Charles Booth produced an intricately coloured map of London, indicating the living conditions of its residents. Dubbed the 'Poverty Map', it offered the following categories to describe each area's inhabitants:

- Upper-middle and Upper classes. Wealthy.
- Middle-class. Well-to-do.
- Fairly comfortable. Good ordinary earnings.
- Mixed. Some comfortable, others poor.
- Poor. 18s to 21s a week for a moderate family.
- Very poor, casual. Chronic want.
- Lowest class. Vicious, semi-criminal.

The full map can be seen at http://booth.lse.ac.uk.

DEATH ON THE UNDERGROUND

The underground became an unofficial hiding-place during the air-raids on London. At first the authorities resisted, but eventually the tubes were run as official shelters. However, this was not without risk, and many deaths ensued, including the following:

Trafalgar Square, 12 October 1940: seven killed when a bomb exploded at the top of the escalator, filling the platforms with earth

Balham, 14 October 1940: 68 killed when a direct hit caused the road to collapse into the tunnel

Bank, 11 January 1941: 56 killed when a bomb exploded in the escalator machine room

Bethnal Green, 3 March 1943: 173 killed when a woman lost her footing at the front of a crowd pouring into the station after an air raid warning. The people behind her piled up on top of each other. Most died from suffocation.

THE LION SERMON

The lion sermon is preached on or about 16 October at St Katharine Cree church, Leadenhall Street, London EC3, and has been every year since 1649. It was started by Sir John Gayer, once Lord Mayor of London and a big cheese in the East India Company. The sermon is so called because Sir John once found himself face to face with a lion while travelling in Arabia. Defenceless, he took a leaf out of Daniel's book and simply fell to his knees and prayed, whereupon the lion, after sizing him up for a while, turned and slunk off. Overcome with gratitude, Sir John bequeathed a large part of his fortune to charity and endowed a sermon in his home parish, to be delivered on the day of his reprieve. His story is retold each time, along with a passage from the Book of Daniel.

INSPIRED BY A WORM

The first tunnel built under the Thames was designed by Marc Isambard Brunel (1769–1849), father of Isambard Kingdom Brunel. Brunel Senior fled the French revolution for New York and then London, and at one point found himself in debtor's prison. While incarcerated, he watched a shipworm bore a hole through a piece of wood by passing the munched-up wood pulp through its body and excreting it as it progressed. Once released, Brunel worked on his observation, and eventually constructed a huge drill with corkscrew blades that passed excavated material down its length as it moved forward, which was used to bore a tunnel from Wapping to Rotherhithe. The tunnel took 18 years to build, and 10 men died during its construction. The East London railway took over the tunnel in 1869, and it now carries the East London Underground line across the river.

When, in centuries past, London was hit by severe winter weather, it was possible for the Thames to freeze so hard that the city's traders could hold a fair on the ice. But the Frost Fairs, as they were called, came about only because of London Bridge. When the 'new' stone bridge was first built in 1176, replacing the old wooden version, its 19 narrow arches slowed the flow of water down so much that the river was able to freeze when temperatures dropped. Although the residents ventured on to the frozen river many times, the first real Frost Fair was not held until 1564, when stalls, sideshows and many forms of entertainment, including merry-go-rounds and donkey races were set up on the ice, which remained frozen for two months. The river froze many times after that, although the Frost Fairs took place only four more times, in 1684, 1716, 1740 and 1814. The last fair began on 1 February, and stretched from Blackfriars to Three Crane Stairs. A 'road' took shape across the river from bank to bank and was temporarily named City Road. Stalls, sideshows and other entertainments were set up, and even a printing press or two was installed to print souvenirs of the great fair. The ice was not entirely safe; one or two people who strayed from the centre of activities fell through cracks in the ice, and a large piece of ice broke off near London Bridge, carrying away a man and two boys. Luckily they lay on the ice, and were soon rescued by some Billingsgate fishermen. Apart from this, the fair passed without incident, lasting a full week until rain set in and the ice began to thaw. When the old London Bridge was replaced in 1831, its new design no longer slowed down the river's flow, and that was the end of the Frost Fairs.

SUGGESTIONS FOR A NEW USE
FOR THE MILLENNIUM DOME

**Real suggestions made by potential purchasers
plus a few ideas from members of the public...**

Hi-tech business park
20,000-seat sports and entertainment venue
National football and athletics stadium to replace Wembley
Biotechnology centre
Sports academy or sports centre for public use
Nightclub (the Ministry of Sound held a New Year
party there at the end of 2000)
New housing development
Hospital
Add ears and a trunk and turn it into a white elephant

DEATH, PLAGUE AND OTHER DISASTERS

On the night of 15 October 1987, a severe storm struck
southern Britain. In a storm that raged more fiercely than
any seen since 1703, 18 people were killed, fifteen million
trees were felled, hundreds of thousands of homes were cut
off from electricity and several ships were stranded, cap-
sized or blown away. Regular weather forecasts had not
warned of a storm as it was thought that the bad weather
front would not further North than the English Channel.
London and south-east England took the brunt of the
storm, as gusts of 70 knots raged for three to four hours.
Gatwick Airport reported gusts of 86 knots. Despite being
referred to as a hurricane, the storm cannot be classified
as such, as Hurricane Force applies only to a wind of 64
knots or more, sustained over at least 10 minutes. Gusts
are not taken into account, even though they cause much
of the destruction. In London, the mean wind speed stayed
below 44 knots.

OVERHEARD ON THE TUBE

Proof that London Underground drivers have a heart, a soul and a sense of humour. In spite of everything.

Northern Line: 'Hello, this is the driver speaking, I am the captain of your train, and we will be departing shortly. We will be cruising at an altitude of approximately zero feet, and our scheduled arrival time in Morden is 3.15pm. The temperature in Morden is approximately 15 degrees celsius, and Morden is in the same time zone as Mill Hill East, so there is no need to adjust your watches.'

Piccadilly Line: 'Please allow the doors to close. Try not to confuse this with "Please hold the doors open." The two are distinct and separate instructions.'

District Line: 'May I remind all passengers that there is strictly no smoking allowed on any part of the Underground. However, if you are smoking a joint, it is only fair that you pass it round the rest of the carriage.'

Jubilee Line (while stuck in a tunnel): 'Well, ladies and gentlemen, I'm pleased to tell you it's a lovely sunny day outside. But of course you wouldn't know that, because you're sitting in the dark.'

Piccadilly Line: 'To the gentleman wearing the long grey coat trying to get on the second carriage, what part of "Stand clear of the doors" don't you understand?'

Waterloo and City: 'Well ladies and gentlemen. I can see a light in front of me which I think is probably Bank Station, so that's good isn't it? But I personally was hoping for Calais. Perhaps next time, eh?'

Piccadilly Line: 'The next stop is Arsenal. For those of you that wish to see Tony Adams standing around for 90 minutes with his arm in the air, please get off here.'

Central Line: 'Ladies and gentlemen, I do apologise for the delay to your service. I know you're all dying to get home, unless, of course, you happen to be married to my ex-wife, in which case you'll want to cross over to the Westbound and go in the opposite direction.'

Central Line: 'Next time, you might find it easier to wait until the doors are open before trying to get on the train.'

At Barking: 'We're sorry for the delay. This is because the train is waiting for a new driver. Not that there was anything wrong with the old one. But we're waiting for a new one.'

Northern Line: 'Ladies and gentlemen, this train has 22 doors on each side, please feel free to use all of them, not just the two in the middle.'

District Line: 'To the hilarious gentleman who just showed me his bum, can I suggest that you join a gym or go on a diet.'

Waterloo and City Line: 'Good evening ladies and gents, and welcome to the Waterloo and City line. Sights to observe on the journey are, to your right, black walls and, to your left, black walls. See the lovely black walls as we make our way to Waterloo. We will shortly be arriving at Waterloo where this train will terminate. We would like to offer you a glass of champagne on arrival and you will notice the platform will be lined with lap-dancers for your entertainment.'

Northern Line: 'Ladies and gentlemen we will shortly be arriving at Waterloo, then I think we will carry right on through the Channel Tunnel and spend the weekend in Paris.'

At Aldgate East station: 'Please use all available doors, there are some really good ones at the front of the train.'

With grateful thanks to www.going-underground.net

OLD PICTURE, NEW CAPTION

No matter the weather, as long as Cliff Richard was in the stands, the players played on.

HIPPOS IN THE THAMES

Eighteen thousand years ago, during the last glacial episode of the Ice Age, most of Britain was covered by ice, during which time woolly mammoths roamed the Thames Valley. At the peak of the Ice Age, the sea-level was 120 metres lower than it is now, and the English Channel and most of the North Sea were land. The Ice Age consisted of glacial and interglacial cycles, and during the interglacials, it was warm enough for hippopotamus, hyena and lions to live in the area that is now London. Hippopotamus bones were discovered during the building of the National Gallery.

WHO WAS THAT MAN?

Just some of the people suspected of being Jack the Ripper, who murdered at least five prostitutes in the Whitechapel area in 1888 and was never caught.

- Joseph Barnett, fish-porter who lived with Mary Jane Kelly, a Ripper victim
- WH Bury, hanged for murdering his wife. Marks left on her body were similar to those on one Ripper victim.
- Prince Albert Victor, Queen Victoria's grandson, supposedly driven insane by syphilis
- Alfred Napier Blanchard, who confessed to the murders while drinking in a pub and was arrested, but was not believed to be telling the truth
- Lewis Carroll, the author of *Alice's Adventures in Wonderland*, who, according to writer Richard Wallace in his 1996 book, scattered clues to his guilt throughout his children's stories
- David Cohen, a Polish Jew, who allegedly hated women and especially prostitutes
- Dr T Neill Cream, abortionist and quack doctor, hanged for murdering several women
- Frederick Deeming, wife-murderer and child-killer
- Montague John Druitt, barrister, who committed suicide around the time of the murders
- Jill the Ripper, an unknown woman supposedly seen wearing one of the victim's clothes
- Severin Klosowski, Polish wife-poisoner
- Walter Sickert, the artist, in a complicated conspiracy theory involving the royal family
- James Kenneth Stephen, friend of Prince Albert Victor
- Francis Tumblety, quack doctor who hated women and kept a collection of wombs in glass jars; the suspect of choice for Scotland Yard
- Nicholas Vassily, Russian anarchist and murderer of prostitutes

GET BACK IN YOUR BOX

Items thrown at illusionist David Blaine when he spent 44 days without food in a perspex box over the Thames in 2003

Eggs
Golf balls
Balloons filled with pink paint
Bananas
Bottles
Chips

Things he threw back (as souvenirs for his fans)

Pencils
Socks
Toilet roll
A strip of black bin liner

Other distracting events

His water supply pipe was cut
Women flashed their breasts at him
He was mooned
People banged drums to keep him awake
Laser pens were shone into the box
A remote control helicopter carrying
a beefburger was flown up to the box

CHURCH ROADS

For centuries, churches were built along ley lines, and people continued to use the ley line as a thoroughfare, walking straight through the centre of the church on their way to somewhere else. St Paul's cathedral was no exception. It was common practice for people taking goods to market to walk right down the aisle, complete with cattle and horses.

LUVVERLY GRAPEFRUIT

Market trader Jack Smith was the first man to introduce the grapefruit to London when he sold it on his fruit stall in Berwick Street Market in 1890.

LONDON BRIDGE IS LEAVING TOWN

In the 1960s the heavy traffic in London meant that the old London Bridge was falling down. Meetings were held by the London council to decide what to do with the bridge, and it was the suggestion of a man named Ivan Luckin that it should be sold to the Americans. As well as being a London councillor, Luckin owned an advertising company and travelled to the United States regularly on business. He told the council that he believed the Americans would be keen to buy the bridge, and to own a piece of English history. His idea was ridiculed, but Luckin was adamant, and visited America with the Town Clerk of London to promote the sale. Four hundred television stations, radio stations and newspapers attended the press conference and the bridge was duly sold in 1968 for $2,460,000 to Robert McCulloch of McCulloch Oil, who had the bridge disassembled, transported and rebuilt in Arizona, where it has become a major tourist attraction. While disdainful Brits like to joke that the oil baron thought he was getting Tower Bridge, Ivan Luckin strongly disputes this rumour. The bridge was further immortalised in the *Guinness Book of Records* as the largest antique in the world to be sold.

CAPITAL CONUNDRUMS

Which tube line best describes its entire function?
Answer on page 144

SONGS ABOUT LONDON THAT
WERE NEVER MADE (SADLY)

Do You Know Edgware You're Going To?
Harrow, I Love You (Won't You Tell Me Your Name)
It's Pinner Hard Day's Night
It's Rainham Men

RIOTING IN THE STREETS

The racial tinderbox that is Brixton in southwest London erupted into violence after a young black man was stopped and searched by police there on Saturday 11 April 1981. Hundreds rampaged through the streets, hurling petrol bombs at police, burning cars and looting shops. The rioting began around Railton Road and Atlantic Road, where there had already been clashes between police and black youths the previous night. As the police began to make arrests, more and more rioters joined the fray and the violence increased faster than the police reinforcements could arrive. More than 50 police officers were injured and around 20 people arrested.

The riot was blamed on police action in the preceding weeks, when Operation Swamp sent police out on the streets to stop and question people at random.

There was a repeat of the violence 14 years later in 1995, when the death of 26-year-old Wayne Douglas in police custody sparked riots in the area. A peaceful picket outside the police station turned into an angry march, when police confronted the protestors and it deteriorated. Shots were heard; a policeman was pulled from his motorbike; and officers sealed off a two-mile area around the centre of Brixton to contain the violence. At the postmortem, Wayne Douglas was found to be suffering from heart disease.

PUB QUIZ

Did you know…?

The Castle,
Cowcross Street EC1
The only pub in England
with a pawnbroker's license.

Hand and Shears,
Middle Street,
Cloth Fair EC1
Prisoners had their cases
heard upstairs and if the
judgment went against
them, they were allowed a
drink at the bar on their
way to the gallows.

Hoop and Grapes,
47 Aldgate High Street EC3
Thirteenth century inn, the
oldest non-ecclesiastical
building in the City.

Ship Tavern,
Lime Street EC3
Built in 1447.

Ship and Blue Ball,
Boundary Road E2
The Great Train Robbery
was planned here in the
Sixties, and, allegedly, a
false wall in the games
room concealed the
stolen millions.

Old Nun's Head,
Nunhead Green SE15
The inn stands on the
site of a nunnery which
was demolished in the
Reformation. The abbess
was decapitated, and her
head displayed on a pole.

Ladbroke Arms,
Ladbroke Road W12
The pub was won by Lord
Ladbroke in payment of a
gambling debt.

The Dove,
Upper Mall W6
Rule Britannia was written
here; Nell Gwynne, Ernest
Hemingway and Graham
Greene drank here; it has
the smallest recorded bar:
4ft 2in by 7ft 10in.

Town of Ramsgate,
Wapping High Street E1
Colonel Blood was
captured here as he tried
to steal the Crown Jewels
from the Tower of London;
the hanging judge, Judge
Jeffries, was also captured
at the Town of Ramsgate.

SMARTER THAN THE AVERAGE

When a taxi driver in London acquires The Knowledge, a demanding test of their familiarity with London's streets, traffic patterns and key attractions, it actually makes him (or her) smarter. The would-be drivers have to memorise 400 'runs' in the so-called Blue Book, requiring instant recall of around 25,000 different thoroughfares within a six-mile radius of Charing Cross, and a general knowledge of the major roads outside that inner circle. The demands that this places on a driver's spatial skills and memory has been shown to have a beneficial effect. A study carried out at University College in London in 2000 showed that learning and using The Knowledge increases the size of the anterior and posterior hippocampi of the brain, the areas that handle spatial memory and spatial navigation. Compared with control groups and less experienced cab drivers, long-serving taxi drivers had considerably more developed hippocampi. So when London cabdriver Fred Housego won 'Mastermind' in 1980, it should not have come as such a surprise.

DOGS IN LONDON

Where our faithful friends will sit and stay for ever more

Two bronze pointers: In the porch of St George's, Hanover Square, W1

Edith Cavell's stuffed dog: Imperial War Museum, SE1

Stone retriever: St Pancras Gardens, NW1

White greyhound: Outside, appropriately enough, The Greyhound, SW16

Appealing puppy: By the dogs' drinking fountain in Kensington Gardens, SW7

Giro: Buried in 1934, the faithful hound once owned by German ambassador Leopold von Hoesch lies in the front garden of 9 Carlton House Terrace, SW1.

NOTORIOUS LONDON PUBS

The Goat, Kensington

Murderer John George Haigh met his first victim, William McSwann, here before luring him off, killing him and dissolving his body in a bath of acid.

IT BEATS AS IT SWEEPS AS IT CLEANS

The vacuum cleaner was invented after a young man named H Cecil Booth witnessed a carpet-cleaning demonstration at an exhibition at London's Empire Music Hall in 1898. Booth watched as a US invention blew dust messily into a box, and he suggested that it might be better if the contraption sucked up the dust. The demonstrator said it couldn't be done – so Booth set out to do it. After experimenting with bits of fabric, through which he sucked up dust from his own carpet, by mouth, Booth found that a closely woven handkerchief worked best. He duly invented a suction cleaner that filtered out the dust, which he patented in 1901. Westminster Abbey, which Booth was employed to tidy up for Edward VII's coronation, was one of the first buildings to be vacuum cleaned. Years of historic dust were duly removed, to the astonishment of the Abbey's own cleaning staff. Booth's machines were also used to clean the dust from Crystal Palace, where an outbreak of scarlet fever was believed to have been caused by infected dust particles. Fifteen machines stripped the building of every last scrap of dust, and the outbreak was quashed. Versions of the machine were developed in Europe and, most famously, in the US by a Mr Spangler, who sold the rights to one William Hoover. Despite the fact that no one now remembers Cecil Booth, it is perhaps just as well; 'I'll run a Booth over it,' doesn't sound quite the same.

WRITING ON THE WALL

Graffiti spotted in London

Good morning, lemmings
Facing commuters on the M4 as they enter London

*God is not dead but alive and well and working
on a much less ambitious project*
On the wall of a Greenwich pub

NICE WORK IF YOU CAN GET IT

A popular way to earn money in late eighteenth-century London was to dig up dead bodies. A body could fetch up to £4, or less for a 'short' (a child). The gravediggers were known as 'resurrection men' and while their victims were unresisting, they did run the risk of being caught by spring guns, primitive land-mines and other booby traps set up by the grieving relatives. The favoured method for a 'resurrection' was to dig a small hole down to the coffin, break the coffin lid and drag the body up through the narrow opening, rather than dig up the entire grave, which took time and attracted attention. Some resurrection men resorted to murder to speed up the process, such as James May and John Bishop. Both were arrested in 1831 after arguing over the price of a body supplied to King's College Hospital, which turned out to be that of a street urchin they had murdered. They were hanged, and their bodies dissected by surgeons.

SPORTING LONDON

The original pitch for the Oval cricket ground in Kennington consisted of 10,000 squares of turf cut from Tooting Common.

LONDON GAMBLERS

Gambling has always been a classless hobby in London, from cockfighting pits to the most exclusive of gentleman's clubs. But it is the latter that saw the greatest gains and losses, as the idle upper classes found a use for their spare time (and spare money).

- In February 1772, **Charles James Fox** lost £11,000 while playing for 24 hours straight at his club, Almack's in Pall Mall. He won back £6,000 two days later, then lost his winnings at Newmarket the same afternoon. He lost a further £10,000 back at Almack's two days later.
- Banker **George Drummond** lost £20,000 in a single game of whist at White's and was forced to resign his position at the family bank.
- **Henry Weston**, 23, resorted to forgery as a means to help clear his gambling debts, and was hanged for the offence in 1796.
- **Lord Robert Spencer**, brother of the Duke of Marlborough, having lost all his money, gambled with a loan and won £100,000, with which he bought an estate in Sussex.
- **Henry Thynne**, also heavily in debt, won back enough in a single night to clear all debts and buy a new house.
- Many gamblers killed themselves after losing everything, including Sir John Bland, Lord Montfort and John Damer, son of Lord Milton.

SOHO SHELTER

The charming little mock-Tudor hut at the centre of Soho Square looks like a very upmarket gardener's shed. It in fact once housed a transformer for the Charing Cross Electric Light Company, and stands over one of the many abandoned underground shelters that were built during World War Two.

LONDON'S BURNING

The early fires of London

Around the year 130, fire swept through London, destroying 100 acres of the city. As most buildings were made of wattle-and-daub and timber, the effects were devastating.

In the seventh century, St Paul's Cathedral, then made of wood, burned down. At the time many houses were built with protruding upper storeys that almost met across the road below, creating a wind tunnel that exacerbated any fire.

To reduce the risk of fire, William the Conqueror introduced a curfew, which meant that all fires and lights had to be extinguished at 8 o'clock every night. But there were two more huge fires in 1077 and 1087, the latter again burning down St Paul's Cathedral.

Further fires came in 1093, 1132 and 1135, the last of which burned down London Bridge. The city's wooden buildings and lack of firefighting equipment – and the belief that a serious fire was an act of God – made fire a constant threat.

In 1212, crowds surged on to London Bridge to watch the first Great Fire of London. But many were trapped when fire spread to the bridge. Few survived the leap into the river below.

Four further big fires followed, and in 1497 Henry VII had to flee Sheen Palace in Richmond when it was destroyed by fire. As the city grew, proper chimneys were installed, although some were made of hollowed tree trunks.

By 1600 the first fire engines were in use, though they were hand-pumped and useful only for small fires. King James I encouraged the use of stone in building, but only a few years after his death, in 1633, a large fire swept across London Bridge and along the riverbank, setting the wooden houses on fire as it went. Several people killed. But the cost was small compared to the terrible fire that was to come.

OLD PICTURE, NEW CAPTION

*While he agreed the traffic in central London
was bad, George thought the new trams were
taking things a step too far*

MIND THE GAP, DEAR

When London architect Mike Kelly left the City for a
new home in Herefordshire, he missed his favourite Tube
trains so much – in which he had ridden since he was a
child – that he took one of them with him. When he heard
that the 1959 rolling stock on the Northern Line was to
be replaced, he tracked down his favourite car, no 1304,
and rescued it from a North London siding. He installed it
in his back garden on a bit of track and it now provides
an interesting and rather unusual venue for afternoon tea
when the weather's nice.

I LEFT IT ON THE BUS

A few things left behind on London Transport

24,084 cases and bags
20,846 books
10,614 mobile phones
7,505 sets of keys
7,026 umbrellas
6,118 pairs of spectacles
2,671 pairs of gloves
474 single gloves
a 14-foot boat
a wedding dress
an urn filled with ashes
several lawyers' robes
a briefcase containing
£10,000
false teeth, limbs and eyes
a lawnmower

a Chinese typewriter
breast implants
a theatrical coffin
a stuffed eagle
a divan bed
an outboard motor
a park bench
a grandfather clock
a bishop's crook
a garden slide
a jar of bull's sperm
a stuffed puffa fish
a vasectomy kit
a harpoon gun
two human skulls in a bag
a kitchen sink

Over 133,000 items are found every year. If an item is not picked up by its owner within three months (money is kept for 12 months), it is sold and the proceeds go towards the running costs of the Lost Property Office.

A STRETCHER THE IMAGINATION

Some of London's railings have more to them than meets the eye. About six feet long and four feet wide, each panel consists of a close metal mesh and, near each corner, the outer rail has been bent outwards in a shallow V-shape. The simple explanation is that these were primitive stretchers used in World War Two – the V-shapes acted as the feet when the stretchers were set down on the ground. The war over, they were used to make fences, as raw materials for rebuilding were, by then, very thin on the ground.

CAPITAL CONUNDRUMS

Who was the first person to have a blue plaque
attached to the house where they had lived?
Answer on page 144

YOUR NAME IN LIGHTS

The neon advertisements of Piccadilly Circus took root before neon was invented, when a set of buildings was demolished at the end of Glasshouse Street in 1886. Though the buildings were intended to improve access to the newly constructed Shaftesbury Avenue, they gave property owners whose buildings now faced directly on to the Circus an idea. Making use of the newly invented electric advertisements, they put illuminated signs on the roofs of their buildings. The London County Council objected on the grounds of vulgarity and managed to get them taken down. But the building owners simply reattached the signs to the front of their buildings instead. The law as it stood did not prevent this, and the council found that it could order the removal of the signs only if they were a threat to pedestrian safety, but when they tried to do so, the courts judged that the signs were safe, and there they have remained ever since. However, many buildings around the Circus are Crown Estate properties, whose leases were better able to prevent the attachment of any such signs to their buildings – which is why the neon boards are concentrated in one or two places rather than filling the whole circus.

LONDON PHRASES

London paste – a paste made of caustic soda and unslacked lime; used as to destroy tumours.

OLDEST RESTAURANT

Rules is the oldest restaurant in London that is still in its original location, on Maiden Lane in Covent Garden. Established by Thomas Rule in 1798, it now serves traditional British food, specialising in game, oysters, pies and puddings. Rules was the favourite spot for Edward VII, when he was still Prince of Wales, for wining and dining his mistress, the actress Lillie Langtry.

LONDON – THE EARLY YEARS

A beginner's guide to London's early history

55 BC	Julius Caesar invades Britain
43 AD	Claudius establishes London and builds the first bridge over the Thames
60	Boadicea attacks and burns London to the ground
200	City wall built
410	Roman troops begin to leave London
604	King Ethelbert builds the first St Paul's Cathedral
834	The Vikings invade
884	Alfred the Great takes power
1014	Olaf invades and pulls down London Bridge
1042	Edward the Confessor becomes king
1065	Westminster Abbey completed
1066	William I is crowned king in the Abbey
1086	Domesday Book is completed
1176	Work begins on the first stone London Bridge – the only bridge across the Thames until 1750
1189	Henry Fitzailwyn becomes London's first mayor
1197	Richard I sells control of the River Thames to the Corporation of London
1240	First Parliament sits at Westminster
1348	Black Death cuts the population by half
1381	Peasants' Revolt
1397	Richard Whittington becomes mayor

Madame Tussaud

Marie Grosholz was born in Strasbourg in 1761 and learned the art of wax modelling Dr Philippe Curtius, her mother's employer. The first likeness she made, in 1777, was of Voltaire. In 1780, she was appointed art tutor to King Louis XVI's sister, and went to live at the royal court in Versailles. When the French Revolution broke out, she was obliged to mould heads of some of the victims of the guillotine, some of whom had been her friends at court. In 1794 she inherited Curtius's collection of figures, and a year later married François Tussaud. Now Madame Tussaud, she took her collection of figures to England in 1802, where she opened her first exhibition at the Lyceum Theatre in London. An instant success, the show toured England and Scotland for 33 years. Marie survived a shipwreck in the Irish Sea and a fire during the Bristol Riots of 1831, and still managed to create new figures to add to the show as she travelled, and finally settling at premises in Baker Street in 1835. After her death in 1850, the exhibition remained at Baker Street until 1884, when her grandsons moved it to its present site in Marylebone Road. The entire collection was nearly destroyed by a fire in 1925, and it took three years to rebuild, reopening with a new cinema and restaurant. A German bomb destroyed the cinema in 1940, and ironically the figure of Hitler was one of the few figures to survive the attack. Madame Tussaud enjoyed one more piece of immortality – she was the inspiration for Mrs Jarley in Charles Dickens's *The Old Curiosity Shop*, and would no doubt have agreed with Mrs Jar-ley's sentiment: 'I won't go so far as to say that, as it is, I've seen waxwork quite like life, but I've certainly seen some life that was exactly like wax-work.'

SONGS ABOUT LONDON THAT WERE NEVER MADE (SADLY)

Esher Really Going Out With Him
Theydon Bois Are Back In Town
Cheam (May Be the Face I Can't Forget)
I Left My Heart in Stamford's Disco
East Sheen She Lovely

THE JOY OF SHEDS

Cabbies' shelters, those oversized green sheds that can occasionally be spotted in the smarter parts of London, were first installed in the interests of road safety. On a rainy day in 1874, Captain George Armstrong, the managing editor of the *Globe* newspaper, couldn't find a cab – or, rather, he could see plenty of cabs but no cabbies. After a little investigation, he found the cabdrivers taking shelter in a nearby pub, and enjoying a beer or two. He concluded that if cabbies had their own shelters, they could enjoy cheaper food and stay away from the temptations of alcohol. Given that Victorian cabbies were notorious for their insobriety, his innovation was well overdue. He set up the Cabmen's Shelter Fund, which built 61 shelters over the next 40 years, containing tables, benches, a small kitchen and a supply of non-alcoholic drinks. Today, sadly, only 13 of these survive, but some will happily sell you a cup of tea and a bacon sandwich, whether you're a cab-driver or not.

CAPITAL CONUNDRUMS

Which two London Underground stations
have all five vowels in their names?
Answer on page 144

STRANGE EXHIBITS

National Army Museum
The frostbitten fingers of an English soldier who climbed Everest in the 1970s

London Canal Museum
Ice wells 100 feet deep, built in 1860 for the ice cream pioneer, Carlos Gatti

Cuming Museum
The leg of an Egyptian mummy, and a tobacco pouch made from the skin of an albatross

Horniman
Three voodoo altars and 7,000 musical instruments

Leighton House
Indoor Arab fountain, c.1870

MCC Museum
Stuffed sparrow and the cricket ball that killed it

Royal London Hospital Archives
A fragment of George Washington's false teeth and a video of the remains of the Elephant Man

Sir John Soane Museum
Egyptian sarcophagus, dated c.1370 BC

Bramah Tea and Coffee Museum
World's largest teapot, which is 32 inches high and 78 inches round and makes 800 cups of tea

Old Operating Theatre Museum
A bit of nineteenth century brain and the original recipe for Snail Water, which was intended to cure venereal disease

Natural History Museum
A walrus from Hudson Bay, overstuffed by a keen London taxidermist in the 1880s

And the one that got away...
London Transport Museum
used to exhibit the remains of a spiral escalator, but it is sadly now 'almost rubble' and kept in their warehouse at Acton

OLD PICTURE, NEW CAPTION

*When he joined the London Zoo volunteer scheme,
Alfred hadn't bargained on being assigned to the
elephant house*

WE'RE JUST MOVING HOUSE

In 1947, a new Ministry of Defence building was scheduled for construction just off Whitehall. The only snag
was that underneath the site was a wine cellar once owned
by Cardinal Wolsey, measuring 32 feet in width, and
20 feet in height. The building could not continue while it
remained, so rather than destroy it, the entire cellar was
temporarily moved out of the way, lock, stock and (appropriately) barrel. The 1000-tonne structure was placed on a
concrete platform, which in turn rested on 200 steel
rollers. The whole was then gently shifted 43 feet and six
inches to the west. The site was excavated by a further
20 feet, and the cellar was rolled back into place, and came
to rest in its original location, 20 feet lower down. The
whole process took around two and a half years.

THE PRESIDENTIAL BUNKER

In his book *Subterranean City*, Antony Clayton tells how, during World War Two, General Eisenhower was given his very own underground shelter. A number of deep-level shelters were built during the war to offer protection from air-raids, and part of the bunker at Goodge Street station was offered to the General in 1942 for his exclusive use. Eisenhower used the shelter as his signal centre during the Normandy landings. However, he actually slept at the Dorchester, which had a gas-proof reinforced concrete basement. After Eisenhower had vacated the shelter, it was used to house British troops on their way to various overseas territories. A fire in 1956 meant that it was abandoned for a while, but in the 1980s it was leased as a storage facility. By 1992, it held tapes of the entire output of Channel 4. The glass mercury arc rectifier that helped to provide emergency lighting was once used to represent an alien brain in an episode of 'Dr Who'.

CLASSIC LONDON TALES

A Journal of the Plague Year, Daniel Defoe (1722)
Oliver Twist, Charles Dickens (1838)
The Old Curiosity Shop, Charles Dickens (1840)
Little Dorrit, Charles Dickens (1857)
Our Mutual Friend, Charles Dickens (1865)
The Europeans, Henry James (1878)
Daisy Miller, Henry James (1879)
Liza of Lambeth, Somerset Maugham (1897)
Hangover Square, Patrick Hamilton (1941)
The Heat of the Day, Elizabeth Bowen (1949)
The End of the Affair, Graham Greene (1951)
The Naked Civil Servant, Quentin Crisp (1968)
The Four-Gated City, Doris Lessing (1969)

COCKNEY

The word 'Cockney' has been used freely, though not always politely, to describe a certain kind of Londoner, chiefly one born in London's East End. The traditional definition of a Cockney is that he or she was born within the sound of the Bow bells, the bells of St Mary-le-Bow, Cheapside. The sound is thought to travel to the City, Bethnal Green, Stepney, Shoreditch, Whitechapel, Finsbury, and all of what is now the borough of Hackney.

The first known use of the term 'Cockney' was around 1600, when Samuel Rowlands in *The Letting of Humours Blood in the Head-Vaine* referred to 'a Bow-bell Cockney'. Some lexicographers attempted to untangle the word in the seventeenth century, but the Oxford English Dictionary later explained that 'cockney' first meant a mis-shapen egg (1362), then a person ignorant of country ways (1521), and then the traditional definition of an East End Londoner.

Cockneys rhyming slang is where everyday words are replaced with a rhyming equivalent, such as 'Barnet Fair' for 'hair'.

However, there is a lost generation of Cockneys. The bells of the church of St Mary-le-Bow were destroyed in the Blitz in 1941 and were not replaced until 1961, so for 20 years, no 'true' Cockneys were born. But really that's just splitting Tony Blairs.

A DAY AT THE ZOO

Some of London Zoo's more unusual residents

moon jellyfish • superb starling • giant frigate beetle
apple snail • blind cave fish • jackass penguin • bongo
okapi • sand cat • kinkajou • toco toucan • bali starling
aye aye • partula snail • komodo dragon • two-toed sloth
spider monkey • audacious jumping spider

A LONDON FIRST

Dulwich Picture Gallery was the first public art gallery in Britain. Its collection was compiled by Sir Francis Bourgeois and Noël Desenfans at the request of the King of Poland. However, when Poland was taken over by Russian and Prussian forces, the king abdicated, leaving Bourgeois and Desenfans with a formidable collection of art but nowhere to exhibit it. Both the British government and the British Museum declined to buy the paintings. Desenfans died in 1807 before the problem was resolved, so when Bourgeois died in 1811 he left the paintings to Dulwich College. His will decreed that they should be accessible to the public, and the Dulwich Picture Gallery was duly founded in the same year to carry out his request. Both Desenfans and Bourgeois are entombed in sarcophagi in the centre of the gallery.

THREE HUNDRED AND FIFTY YEARS LATER...

In 1654, Oliver Cromwell began the process of granting livery status to London cab drivers. But as civil unrest grew, the process was never completed, and the cab drivers' livery status remained in limbo until the 1980s. Then cab driver Phil Warren discovered this little known oversight and began to write about it, which encouraged a group of taxi drivers to finish the long process of becoming a fully fledged Livery company. In 1990, cab drivers were granted Fellowship status by the City of London, and seven years later – the required waiting time – they were declared a Company and were able to apply for full Worshipful status. This was finally granted in 2004, making cab drivers the 104th livery company in London – the Worshipful Company of Hackney Cab Drivers.

LONDON ON LOCATION

Films shot in and around Covent Garden:

- *The Red Shoes* (1948): the Royal Opera House provides the backdrop for the opening scenes.
- *Modesty Blaise* (1966): the heroine is lured out of retirement while at the Royal Opera House.
- Hitchcock's *Frenzy* (1972) was shot in the old Covent Garden, when it was still an open market selling flowers, fruit and vegetables.
- *Scenes from Travels with my Aunt* (1972) were shot in the Lamb and Flag pub in Rose Street, and the aunt's flat was shot above the Salisbury pub in St Martin's Lane.
- In *Four Weddings and a Funeral* (1994), Andie MacDowell and Hugh Grant swop ex-lover statistics in the Dome restaurant in Wellington Street.
- The climactic scene in *Notting Hill* (1999) takes place in the Savoy Hotel, as Hugh Grant gatecrashes the press conference.
- In *Billy Elliott* (2000), his father and brother travel to London to see him perform, and arrive late at the Theatre Royal, Drury Lane.
- Somerset House has appeared in numerous films, and not always as itself; Edward Fox acquired a false birth certificate there in *The Day of the Jackal* (1973); in *Goldeneye* (1995) it doubled for St Petersburg, and became MI6 headquarters in *Tomorrow Never Dies* (1997). It became a turn-of-the-century New York building in *Sleepy Hollow* (1999), the exterior of Oscar Wilde's apartment in *Wilde* (1998) and a Russian building attacked by Bolsheviks in *Reds* (1981). It also played bit parts in *The Secret Agent* (1995), *Sense and Sensibility* (1995) and *Black Beauty* (1994).
- The one film that should have been set in Covent Garden – *My Fair Lady* – where Eliza Doolittle sold her flowers, was shot in a studio.

HISTORY IN THE NURSERY

The clock on the church of St Clement Danes plays the tune of the famous nursery rhyme 'Oranges and Lemons', which is appropriate, as it is the first church mentioned in the rhyme:

> *Oranges and lemons*
> *Say the bells of St Clements;*
> *You owe me five farthings*
> *Say the bells of St Martin's;*
> *When will you pay me?*
> *Say the bells of Old Bailey;*
> *When I grow rich*
> *Say the bells of Shoreditch;*
> *When will that be?*
> *Say the bells of Stepney;*
> *I do not know*
> *Says the great bell of Bow*
> *Here comes a candle to light you to bed*
> *Here comes a chopper to chop off your head*
> *Chop chop chop chop the last man's head!*

The churches mentioned are, in order of appearance:

> St Clements, Eastcheap
> St Martin Orgar, Cannon Street
> St Sepulchre without Newgate
> St Leonards, Shoreditch
> St Dunstan and All Saints, Stepney
> St Mary le Bow, Cheapside

LONDON PHRASES

London Particular – blankets of fog that choked London's air until the Clean Air act was introduced; also the name of a recipe for thick pea and ham soup; and the subtitle of a small London fanzine, *Smoke: A London Particular*.

On 30 April 1980, six Iranian dissidents seized the Iranian Embassy in Prince's Gate, SW1, overpowering the unfortunate constable who stood guard at the door. The six armed men claimed to be from the Democratic Revolutionary Front for Arabistan, and seized the embassy to protest against the oppression of Iran by Ayatollah Khomeini, and to secure the release of 91 imprisoned comrades. Twenty-six people were held hostage for six days, consisting mostly of embassy staff, but including two BBC journalists who had stopped by to pick up visas and got the scoop of a lifetime, though were powerless to do much at the time. Initially the siege was peaceful; some hostages were released, including a pregnant woman and BBC journalist Chris Cramer, who, with the agreement of his fellow hostages, exaggerated a stomach complaint in order to be released. Once out, he provided the SAS with crucial information about the hostage-takers and the layout of the building. The siege dragged on for five long days, but when an Iranian hostage was shot and his body pushed outside, the SAS went in. The storming of the embassy has earned its place in history largely because it took place on Bank Holiday Monday, and was watched live on television by an enthralled public. It was all over in 15 minutes; five of the gunmen and another hostage was killed. PC Trevor Lock, who had been on guard outside and was one of the hostages – was awarded the George Cross for tackling one of the gunmen. The Iranian Embassy remained closed for years while the Iranian and British governments wrangled over who would pay for the damage to the building. It finally reopened in 1993. The five gunmen were buried in Woodgrange Park, Manor Park, in an unmarked grave.

LONG AGO, BEFORE
THE DAYS OF KFC...

In 1172, Londoner William FitzStephen wrote an extended essay on the many delights of London, which included a description of perhaps the first London takeaway. On the river-bank he saw a public cook-shop selling 'seasonal foods, dishes roast, fried and boiled, fish of every size, meat for the poor and delicate for the rich, such as venison and various kinds of birds.'

FitzStephen suggested that it was the perfect solution for when unexpected guests dropped in and there was nothing in the house, that while servants brought the bread, someone could nip down to the river bank and pick up supper. Just the thing – 'since every sort of delicacy is set out for them here'.

SALE OF THE CENTURY

One of the most talked-about auctions in the history of Sotheby's in London was the Goldschmidt sale of 1958. The Goldschmidt collection contained seven of the most exquisite Impressionist and Modern paintings ever to come to auction. The auction house decided to revive an eighteenth century tradition and hold an evening auction, at which the attendants were required to wear evening dress. Fourteen hundred people attended, including W Somerset Maugham, Anthony Quinn, Kirk Douglas and Lady Churchill, as well as art dealers from all over the world. All seven pictures were sold in just 21 minutes and fetched £781,000, the highest total ever achieved at the time for a fine art sale. The highest price was paid for Cézanne's *Garçon au Gilet Rouge*, which was sold for £220,000, more than five times the price ever paid for a painting sold at auction. The Goldschmidt sale was one of the social highlights of the year.

SMOKIN'!

The all-American Marlboro brand of cigarettes was named after the Philip Morris factory, which in 1902 was situated on Marlborough Street.

THE REAL LONDON BRIDGE

Various wooden bridges have stood on or near the site of the current London Bridge since before Roman times, but in 1176 a cleric called Peter de Colechurch, decided to build a revolutionary stone bridge. It took 33 years to build, and consisted of 19 arches, which stretched 900 feet across the Thames. It was paid for by a tax levied by Henry II on wool, which gave rise to the saying 'London Bridge was built upon woolpacks'.

Peter de Colechurch died before the bridge was completed, and was suitably buried in the crypt contained within the bridge. But his pioneering bridge stood for 655 years before it was defeated by the growing volume of London traffic, and demolished to make way for a bigger, stronger construction. However, its successor, designed by John Rennie lasted only 140 years before it had to be replaced again, thanks once more to the pressures of traffic and population. An arch of the original wooden bridge could be found in the Museum of London, and an arch of the Rennie Bridge lives in Kew Gardens. Two of the stone structures that were on the bridge were displayed in Victoria Park, Hackney, by St Augustine's Gate.

CAPITAL CONUNDRUMS

Which famous writer's portrait in the
National Portrait Gallery is the only one
of him known to be painted from life?
Answer on page 144

OLD PICTURE, NEW CAPTION

*Mrs Biggins spent days perfecting the correct
approach for getting exactly what she wanted
at the Harrods' sale*

TOP TEN TOWERS

The ten tallest towers in London

One Canada Square	50 floors	244m (800ft)
8 Canada Square	45 floors	200m (655ft)
25 Canada Square	45 floors	200m (655ft)
Telecom Tower	43 floors	191m (625ft) (inc mast)
Tower 42	43 floors	183m (600ft)
30 St Mary Axe ('The Gherkin')	41 floors	180m (590ft)
One Churchill Place	33 floors	156m (513ft)
25 Bank Street	33 floors	153m (502ft)
40 Bank Street	33 floors	153m (502ft)
10 Upper Bank Street	32 floors	151m (495ft)

THIRTY-FOUR USES
FOR AN ALBERT HALL

**A few events that have taken place
in London's roundest concert hall**

- **1872** Demonstration of Morse apparatus by the Society of Telegraph Engineers and Commissioners
- **1881** First ball held, by the Chelsea Hospital for Women
- **1888** First dinner held, for 1400 guests who dined in the amphitheatre and arena, with more in the balconies and boxes
- **1889** Ice Carnival, Bazaar and Festival, including an ice sculpture of the palace of Montreal and snow shoe races
- **1891** Albert Hall registered as a place of worship
- **1895** Salvation Army hold their first rally at the hall
- **1908** First Amateur Boxing Competition
- **1909** Marathon is run indoors: 26 miles and 385 yards was equal to 524 circuits of the arena
- **1912** Titanic Band Memorial Concert, conducted by Sir Edward Elgar, Henry Wood, Landon Ronald and Thomas Beecham
- **1941** The first Proms season
- **1943** Secret Government 'pep-talk' on war work for women, with Churchill, Attlee, Eden, Bevin, Cripps and others speaking
- **1951** The Kray twins and Charlie Kray take part in a public boxing match
- **1968** Eurovision Song Contest
- **1971** Muhammad Ali boxes
- **1991** FW de Klerk declares apartheid dead

LONDON PHRASES

London plane – a hybrid plane tree, resistant to smoke and therefore often planted in streets.

When in 1660 Charles II regained the throne that had been taken from his father, the immorality of his court caused many to predict that a terrible judgment would be visited upon him, and the date often mentioned was 1666, as 666 was the devil's number.

In September 1666, the city was tinder-dry after a long drought, and the fire that famously started at a baker's in Pudding Lane on 1 September took hold quickly. The Mayor, Sir Thomas Bludworth, not only underestimated the seriousness of the fire but also would not authorise the pulling down of four houses to act as a firebreak, as he was worried about who would pay for the rebuilding.

It was, in fact, Samuel Pepys who went to the king and insisted that he intervene and order the mayor to create a firebreak. Charles gave the order, but the fire burned on. People scattered from the city with their belongings in carts, and suspected arsonists were beaten in the streets. The fire burned from Saturday night until Wednesday, until the wind finally dropped and the firefighters were able to bring the blaze under control. Around 436 acres of London were destroyed and only 75 acres saved. One in three houses burned down, as well as many important and historic buildings, such as the Royal Exchange and Newgate Prison. The city lost 87 churches, 44 livery halls and 13,200 houses. And while 70,000 people were made homeless, the most astonishing statistic of the fire was the death toll – only six people perished. By 11 September, Christopher Wren had already submitted plans for rebuilding the city. A Frenchman, Robert Hubert, claimed to have pushed fireballs through the window of the bakery and was held responsible for starting the fire. No one believed he was guilty, but he was hanged anyway.

Pubs full of a different kind of spirit...

**The Mitre,
Craven Terrace W2**
Haunted by the ghost of a
coachman who lived in the
stables, which were where
the cellar bar now is.

**Rose & Crown,
Old Park Lane W1**
Most haunted pub in
London, because prisoners
heading for Tyburn gallows
were often incarcerated in
the cellars overnight.

**John Snow,
39 Broadwick Street W1**
Named after a surgeon
who helped to quell an
outbreak of cholera in the
area in the nineteenth
century, thanks to his
research into waterborne
disease. An image of the
village water-pump appears
now and then to remind
drinkers to stick to beer.

**Cheshire Cheese,
Little Essex Street WC2**
Jacobean and haunted by a
very strong ghost who
moves the fruit machine.

**Grenadier,
Wilton Row, SW1**
Once the officers' mess for
the Duke of Wellington's
soldiers; the Duke's
mounting block was kept
outside. It is haunted by an
officer who was flogged for
cheating at cards, leading
to his accidental death.

**Crockers,
Aberdeen Place NW8**
Haunted by its founder. He
wrongly believed that trains
from Marylebone would
stop nearby; the custom he
expected never materialised.

**The Bedford,
Bedford Hill SW12**
Haunted by Dr James
Gully, wrongly convicted in
the room upstairs.

**Morpeth Arms,
Millbank SW1**
The cellars connect with a
tunnel used by prisoners to
escape from the Millbank
Penitentiary. Said to be
haunted by those who
didn't make it out.

A FOGGY DAY IN LONDON TOWN

On 5 December 1952, a thick yellow fog descended on London, acrid enough to make the residents' eyes water. Thanks to a warm air front that settled over the Thames valley, the fog hung in the city for four or five days, as the warm air trapped the fog underneath it. Four thousand people died of lung-related problems during the following month, and 12,000 people died overall in a four-month period following the fog, although these figures were denied by the authorities. London had had a history of dense fogs since the start of the industrial revolution, but this one was by far the worst. The fog was so thick that emergency services had to drive around with a policeman walking in front, brandishing a flare. The fog seeped into homes and buildings, and coated everything it touched with a grey film. A performance of *La Traviata* was stopped because the audience could no longer see the stage. At that time, Britain was on the verge of bankruptcy, so the government was exporting the good coal overseas, leaving Britons to burn poorer, smoky coal on their fires. London also had three major power stations in built-up areas, burning coal to produce electricity. The dense fogs continued until the Clean Air Act was finally passed in 1956. It seems rather ironic that the coal tax, imposed to finance the rebuilding of London after the Great Fire of 1666, was placed on the one substance that made the reconstructed city almost uninhabitable.

LONDON SONGS

'London Nights' – *London Boys*
'London Kid' – *Jean Michel Jarre featuring Hank Marvin*
'London Bridge is Falling Down' – *nursery rhyme*
'Streets of London' – *Ralph McTell*

SIGNIFICANT STATUES

Eros

Eros, the monument that lends a little romance to neon-lit Piccadilly Circus, is not in fact Eros, the God of Love, but is actually the Angel of Christian Charity. And it's not really a statue, but a memorial fountain. Erected in 1893 in memory of the Victorian philanthropist Lord Shaftesbury, it has become a resting place and photo-opportunity for tired tourists and courting couples. It was given the name Eros within days of its unveiling in June 1893, not least because the sculptor, Sir Arthur Gilbert, said that it represented 'the blindfolded love sending forth his missile of kindness'. Gilbert meant Christian love, but the naked, Cupid-like figure seems to represent the more earthly kind. The figure itself used to be golden, but the original was replaced by a lead copy. The shooting of an arrow is supposed to be a pun on Shaftesbury – the angel is aiming down to 'bury' the 'shaft' of the arrow in the ground.

The memorial nearly ruined its sculptor; originally planned as a drinking fountain, Gilbert wanted to make it bigger so it was easier to drink from. But the London County Council disagreed, even though it was criticised for its size when it was unveiled (and Gilbert got the blame). Had he had his way, it would be a much more impressive object, with the angel floating apparently unsupported above the fountain. Instead, Gilbert claimed that it traumatised the rest of his life.

CAPITAL CONUNDRUMS

Which Londonite am I?
GSLIVT
E
Answer on page 144

BOOKS WITH LONDON TITLES

Liza of Lambeth, Somerset Maugham, *1897*
The Napoleon of Notting Hill, GK Chesterton, *1904*
Psmith in the City, PG Wodehouse, *1910*
London Belongs To Me, Norman Collins, *1945*
The Ballad of Peckham Rye, Muriel Spark, *1960*
84 Charing Cross Road, Helene Hanff, *1970*
London Fields, Martin Amis, *1989*

RIOTING IN THE STREETS

In 1381, people held a protest against the hated poll tax which was levied by John of Gaunt on every citizen over the age of 15, including the poorest peasants, to pay for the Hundred Years' War. In what became known as the Peasants' Revolt, ex-soldier Wat Tyler led a band of 10,000 peasants to London, stopping off to attack and plunder anything connected with tax collection. Tyler and his band soon reached London Bridge and poured across the river to attack the north bank, joining forces with other rebels from Essex. John of Gaunt's Savoy Palace was relieved of its treasures and burned to the ground. The mob ran out of control, looting and burning buildings and murdering people in the streets. They were eventually calmed by 14-year-old King Richard II, who offered concessions such as fair rents and the abolition of serfdom. However, the rebels were not yet won over, and the next day they captured the King's Treasurer and Archbishop Sudbury and executed them. But when Wat Tyler was killed the following day, the king turned on the rebels, announced that serfdom would not be abolished, and dared the rebels to defy him. A few did, but were swiftly dispatched by the king's men. The revolt was over.

IMPRESSIONS OF LONDON

Just some of Canaletto's many paintings of London

'Westminster Bridge from the
North on Lord Mayor's Day', *1746*
'Seen through an Arch of Westminster Bridge',
1746–1747
'Whitehall and the Privy Garden
from Richmond House', *1747*
'The Thames and the City of London
from Richmond House', *1747*
'Westminster Bridge, London, with the Lord Mayor's
Procession on the Thames', *1747*
'Westminster Abbey', *1748*
'Westminster Abbey, with a Procession of
Knights of the Bath', *1749*
'The Old Horse Guards and Banqueting Hall,
from Saint James' Park', *1749*
'The Old Horse Guards from Saint James' Park', *1749*
'Northumberland House', *1752*
'Greenwich Hospital from the North Bank
of the Thames', *c.1753*
'Ranelagh, Interior of the Rotunda', *1754*
'St Paul's Cathedral, London', *1754*

LONDON LEGENDS

Norman Balon was until recently landlord of the Coach
and Horses, Soho, favourite drinking-place of the late
Jeffrey Barnard, and meeting place for *Private Eye* and the
Oldie. He was known for his irascibility and intolerance of
customers who fell short of his high standards, who were
swiftly thrown out. This was not the result of his drinking
his profits, as he was teetotal. Described as 'crapulous' by
one author, who implied that he was in a sorry, drunken
state, he sued for libel and the book was withdrawn.

I'M A FREE MAN

The granting of the Freedom of the City dates back to the early thirteenth century. A freeman was someone who was not the property of a feudal lord and enjoyed privileges such as the right to earn money and own land, essential for anyone who wanted to practise a trade. Freemen enjoyed a number of other privileges, including the right:

- to herd sheep over London Bridge
- to carry a drawn sword in the City
- to avoid being press-ganged
- to be married in St Paul's Cathedral
- to be buried in the City
- to be drunk and disorderly without fear of arrest
- if convicted of a suitable offence, to be hanged with a silken rope
- if their children were orphaned, to have them educated free of charge at the Freeman's School in Kent
- if they became destitute in old age, to be housed in an almshouse

The freedom of the city is still granted to around 1,800 people a year who meet the criteria, which include being the child or the apprentice of a freeman, or being nominated, usually by the Livery company to which the candidate belongs. In addition, the Corporation of London can invite certain people to be an Honorary Freeman, an honour most recently bestowed upon Winston Churchill, General Eisenhower, Nelson Mandela, cricketer Darren Gough and the late Princess of Wales (female freemen are referred to as 'free sisters').

Only the last two of the special privileges listed above still apply, but the others can be invoked from time to time. In 1983, Freeman Michael Bradshaw exercised his right to drive a flock of sheep over London Bridge. The stunt was in aid of the National Advertising Benevolent Society.

OLD PICTURE, NEW CAPTION

*A traffic warden patiently explains the concept
of a red route to some bemused tourists*

MADE IN LONDON

In 1837, William Fothergill Cooke and Professor Charles
Wheatstone patented a five-needle **telegraph**. On 25 July,
Wheatstone's and Cooke's telegraph was demonstrated
to the directors of the London and Birmingham Railway
between Euston and Camden Town, a distance of just
under a mile. In 1839 the world's first commercial telegraph line using the Cooke and Wheatstone system was
built between Paddington and West Drayton, a distance of
13 miles. It was working to Hanwell by the 6 April and
was completed to West Drayton on 9 April. The public
could pay one shilling to view the telegraph and could
send their own telegrams. In 1845 the first public telegraph
line was opened and ran between London and Gosport.
The first communication transmitted was Queen Victoria's
speech at the opening of Parliament.

THE CULTURAL COALMAN

Cultural life in London in the early 1700s was much encouraged by a humble coalman called Thomas Britton. Arriving in London in 1677, he established a coal business in Clerkenwell Green, living over 'the shop', and it was in his simple rooms that he held musical evenings every week for 40 years. The concerts attracted the likes of Handel as well as society leaders and dignitaries, who enjoyed a very high standard of entertainment, including a few turns by Handel on the five-stop organ. Britton also collected rare books and was helped in his business by the Earls of Oxford and Winchelsea, who would take their finds to a bookshop in Paternoster Row, where Britton would meet them after he had finished shifting his bags of coal. Britton's expertise and interest was such that he helped to form the Harleian Library, which became part of the British Library. Sadly, he was killed by a practical joke in which a ventriloquist pretended to be the voice of God and warned Britton that he would die unless he recited the Lord's Prayer immediately. The superstitious coal merchant was taken ill and died a few days later. His portrait hangs in the National Gallery – in which he is dressed as a coalman.

SONGS ABOUT LONDON THAT WERE NEVER MADE (SADLY)

Acton Baby
Thank Kew For The Music
Sydenham the Dock of the Bay
Tooting Bec to Happiness
Morden A Feeling
Purple Hayes
Sexual Ealing

BRITISH LIBRARY

Facts and figures about the British Library that will please the librarian in all of us

- It receives a copy of every publication produced in the UK and Ireland
- The collection includes 150 million items, in most known languages, dating from 300 BC to the present day
- Three million new items are incorporated every year
- It holds manuscripts, maps, newspapers, magazines, prints and drawings, music scores, and patents
- The Sound Archive keeps everything from sound recordings from nineteenth-century cylinders to the latest CD, DVD and minidisc recordings
- The collection includes 310,000 manuscript volumes, from Jane Austen to the Beatles
- It houses eight million stamps and other philatelic items
- It holds 49.5 million patents
- It holds over four million maps
- It holds over 260,000 journal titles
- The shelf space grows by 12 kilometres every year
- A person inspecting five items a day would take 80,000 years to see the whole of the collection
- It carries out six million searches a year generated by the online catalogue
- Around half a million people visit the reading rooms each year
- Its key possessions include the Magna Carta, the Lindisfarne Gospels, the first dated printed book, *The Diamond Sutra*, Leonardo da Vinci's Notebook, the first edition of *The Times* from 18 March 1788 and the recording of Nelson Mandela's trial speech
- The new building at St Pancras was the largest public building to be constructed in the UK in the twentieth century, and required 10 million bricks and 180,000 tonnes of concrete

YOU CAN TAKE A HORSE TO WATER

Until 1859 it was very difficult for Londoners to find a drink of water without paying for it; and even more difficult for cart drivers and cabbies to find a watering-place for their horses. The only option was to use the troughs of water put out by publicans, but you had to pay a penny – or buy a beer. At this time, there were around 50,000 horses in constant use in the capital, which made a nice living for the pub-owners.

To solve the problem, Samuel Gurney, a member of parliament and Quaker, set up the Metropolitan Free Drinking Fountain Association, opening the capital's first drinking fountain on 21 April 1859. This fountain can still be seen in the wall of St Sepulchre's Church in Newgate Street, EC1. More fountains were installed at a rate of about one a week for about two years, many of which incorporated small drinking-bowls for dogs.

Then in 1867 the Association expanded its activities to include horses and cattle, and changed its name to the Metropolitan Drinking Fountain and Cattle Trough Association. They installed large metal water troughs all over London, which were later replaced by granite, many of which survive today, as does the Association. It is now based in Kent, and installs drinking fountains in schools and playing fields, and works in other countries such as Africa to improve their access to water.

WALKING TO WORK

In 1327, Edward III granted market rights to the City of London in a charter that prohibited the setting up of rival markets within 6.6 miles of the City. This very specific distance was the furthest a person could be expected to walk to market, sell his produce and return in a day.

CAPITAL CONUNDRUMS

Why is the spire of St Bride's eight feet too short?
Answer on page 144

SWAN-UPPING

The swans on the Thames are jointly owned by the reigning monarch and two of the City Livery Companies, the Vintners and the Dyers, a privilege that has existed for 600 years. The swans have always been protected by draconian laws: in the mid-nineteenth century one could be transported for seven years for harming a swan; and even by the end of the century the penalty would still earn the culprit seven weeks' hard labour. Once a year in July, the rightful owners gather at the side of the Thames to count, mark and pinion (clip the wings) the season's new cygnets. The Dyers' swans are marked with one notch to the upper beak, the Vintners' swans have two notches. The Queen's swans are unmarked.

Swan upping probably refers to the fact that the swans have to be taken out of the water to be marked. The ceremony is conducted by three Swan Herdsmen and their teams of Swan Uppers, who row from Temple Stairs to Henley, their boats decorated with their Livery banners. As the boats approach Windsor Castle, the occupants stand to attention and salute 'Her Majesty the Queen, Seigneur of the Swans'. Also, the newest member of the team, known as the colt, is ducked in the river at some point in the proceedings.

FARE ENOUGH

London taxi-drivers are permitted to urinate in public, as long as a member of the police force acts as a witness.

LONDON ROADS

When the powers-that-be were naming some of London's roads, it seems that their minds may have been on more distant locations...

Abyssinia Close, *SW11*

Bangalore Street, *SW15*

Cuba Street, *E14*

Dakota Gardens, *E6*

Edinburgh Road, *W7*

Falkland Avenue, *N11*

Geneva Drive, *SW9*

Hobart Close, *N20*

Iceland Road, *E3*

Jersey Road, *E11*

Khyber Road, *SW11*

Lindisfarne Road, *SW20*

Madeira Road, *N13*

North Pole Road, *W10*

Ontario Street, *SE1*

Perth Avenue, *NW9*

Quebec Way, *SE16*

Rawalpindi House, *E16*

South Africa Road, *W12*

Toronto Road, *E11*

Ulster Terrace, *NW1*

Virginia Street, *E1*

Wales Close, *SE15*

Yukon Road, *SW12*

Zealand Road, *E3*

LONDON PHRASES

London dispersion forces – the forces that exist in nonpolar molecules that involve an accidental dipole that induces a momentary dipole in a neighbour.

GHOSTS AND THE CITY

London is alleged to be awash with ghosts,
all haunting the scenes of their demise.
Here are a few of the many lost souls:

Bank
Haunted by the Bank
Nun, whose brother was
executed 200 years ago
for dealing in forged bank
notes. His grieving sister
now waits for ever for
his return.

Bank Station
When this station was
built, the work disturbed
a graveyard, and staff
have reported feelings of
dread and strange smells
– like that of a newly
opened grave.

British Museum
Haunted by a Priestess of
the Temple of Amen-Ra.
The evil spirits are said to
emanate from a coffin lid
in the Egyptian Room.

Covent Garden Station
Haunted by William
Terriss, who was murdered
in Maiden Lane in 1897.
Staff are often excused from
working there at night.

Farringdon Station
Haunted by the screams of
Anne Naylor, aged 13, who
was murdered in 1798 in a
milliner's shop near to the
station's site.

Hampton Court
Hit the headlines in 2003
when CCTV footage cap-
tured the movements of a
ghostly figure.

North Kensington
Haunted by a driverless
ghostly bus so lifelike that
it has forced motorists off
the road. Has not been
seen since alterations to a
junction on St Mark's
Road made the road safer.

Old Bailey
This stands on the site
of Newgate prison and
is said to be haunted by
a prisoner in the form of a
snarling hound, who was
killed and eaten by his
fellow prisoners, crazed
with starvation.

St James's Palace
Haunted by a Mr Sellis, the valet of the Duke of Cumberland. Sellis's daughter killed herself after she was impregnated by the Duke. Sellis's throat was cut, perhaps to stop him from spilling the beans or from taking revenge.

St Thomas's Hospital
Haunted by a middle-aged lady in a grey uniform, who appears to those who are about to die.

Theatre Royal, Drury Lane
The pale figure of a man with a tricorn hat has been seen in the fourth row of the upper circle. A sighting of him during rehearsals is supposed to bode well for the success of the show.

Westminster Abbey
The ghost of a soldier has been seen standing over the Tomb of the Unknown Soldier, guarding its fallen comrade.

TOWERING FACTS

- The Tower of London was built by William the Conqueror in the eleventh century.
- Its original English name was the White Tower from the Celtic Bryn Gwyn; 'gwyn' means white or pure, 'bryn' means hill.
- The Tower was built on an ancient site, where a sacred mound once stood.
- It was believed that two former British kings were buried under the mound: Brutus (the reputed founder of London) in 1100 BC and Molmutius, buried around 500 BC.
- Malory, in *Le Morte D'Arthur*, says that Guinevere took refuge here to avoid marriage to Sir Mordred.
- It is thought that a 150-foot Roman well sits beneath the Tower, possibly built for astronomical observations, as the deep hole cuts out any glare from the moon.
- The round turret at one corner of the White Tower was used as an observatory until the seventeenth century.

THE RIGHT WAY TO DRIVE

The only place in London where one must drive on the right is when turning off the Strand and into the forecourt of the Savoy. The simple explanation is that the turn off the Strand is too sharp for cars to stay on the left, and entering on the right caused fewer scrapes.

RIOTING IN THE STREETS

On 4 October 1936, Oswald Mosley set off to lead a crowd of anti-Jewish protesters from the Tower of London to the East End, to mark the fourth anniversary of the founding of the British Union of Fascists. Two thousand BUF supporters, known as Blackshirts, congregated around Cable Street, while 500 anti-fascists assembled at the end of Whitechapel High Street to block their way and shouted 'They shall not pass!' Both sides surged towards each other, carrying crude weapons made of bits of wood, and the anti-Fascists overturning vehicles to impede the blackshirts progress. By 3pm the clash had become a pitched battle, with some of the most vicious street fighting ever seen in London. Mosley joined the battle in his Bentley, surrounded by muscled bodyguards. The crowds were eventually dispersed, though not before Mosley made a speech, accusing the government of surrendering to Jewish corruption. The government banned the BUF in 1940 and Mosley was interned for most of the rest of the war. He never successfully returned to politics and eventually moved to France.

CAPITAL CONUNDRUMS

What do Bow Street, Marlborough Street
and Vine Street have in common?
Answer on page 144

OUT OF TOWN

Not every famous London resident had a posh address...

- Sir Ernest Henry Shackleton lived at 12 Westwood Hill, SE26
- Sir Noel Coward lived at 131 Waldegrave Road, Teddington
- William Heath-Robinson lived at 75 Moss Lane, Pinner
- Samuel Taylor Coleridge lived in Dagnall Park, South Norwood, SE25
- William Bligh lived at 100 Lambeth Road, Lambeth, SE1
- John Logie Baird lived at 3 Crescent Wood Road, Sydenham, SE26
- Joseph Chamberlain lived in Camberwell Grove, Camberwell, SE5

LONDON'S BURNING

In the Middle Ages, the amount of tax that a person had paid was recorded on a tally stick, in which notches were made for each payment. The stick was then split in half lengthways, and the government kept the other identically notched half, as a record. The government's halves were piled up over the centuries in the Palace of Westminster, as no one knew what else to do with them. It wasn't until 1834 that someone suggested they could perhaps be got rid of. They were duly burned in a furnace under the House of Lords, but unfortunately the furnace was overloaded and then left to burn unsupervised. It quickly set fire to the rest of the tally sticks and burned down most of the Palace. It also destroyed some historic documents, such as the warrant for the execution of Charles I. The event was immortalised in Turner's painting, 'The Burning of the Houses of Parliament'.

Monument is the tallest freestanding stone column in the world, measuring 202 feet high, and stands close to the site of the baker's house in Pudding Lane where the Great Fire of London began in 1666. The column was designed as a commemoration of the fire by Robert Hooke and Christopher Wren, the two men responsible for rebuilding much of London after the devastating blaze. Made of Portland stone, it took six years to build and was completed in 1677. The ornament for the top is a simple copper urn with gilt flames, which was chosen in preference to Wren's earlier suggestions of a phoenix and a statue of Charles II (the King himself preferred the urn). Inside is a cantilevered stone staircase around a central well with 311 steps leading to a viewing platform 160 feet above ground level. After a number of suicides, the platform was enclosed in 1842. The steps continue

inside the pillar above the platform, and there is a vertical ladder through the urn to a trapdoor at the very top of the Monument.

The Monument was also designed as the setting for a series of experiments that required a structure of some height, and there is a cellar laboratory below the ground floor. Hooke wanted to use the tower to experiment with a zenith telescope, which would make exact measurements of a selected fixed star. The hollow shaft could be opened to the night sky by a hinged trapdoor in the urn at the top, while the experimenter took up his position in the cellar laboratory.

In addition, the steps were built so that each stair-riser was exactly six inches high, so that the tower could be used for experiments on pressure, while the vertical shaft could be used for experiments with pendulums. Hooke duly recorded a number of experiments at the 'Fish Street pillar'.

Bringing his own costume to set, Richard Gere clearly hadn't propery read the script of An Officer and a Gentleman.

DEATH, PLAGUE AND OTHER DISASTERS

London's worst Tube crash took place in February 1975 at Moorgate station. The 8.37am from Drayton Park overshot the platform and crashed at 30mph into a dead-end tunnel at 8.46am. The driver and 42 passengers were killed, and 74 were injured. The cause of the crash was a mystery; the driver was in good health with an unblemished record and had not taken drugs or alcohol. But the guard said that he felt the train speed up as it entered the station, and investigations showed that the brakes were never applied and the driver did not appear to have put his hands up to shield himself before the impact. There appeared to be nothing wrong with the train, signals or track. The cause has never been established.

CAPITAL CONUNDRUMS

The answers. As if you needed them.

P8   The Circle Line

P15   Samuel Pepys

P26   Coventry Street, Glasshouse Street, Piccadilly, Regent Street and Shaftesbury Avenue

P33   They are all called George.

P45   It's the only tube station not to contain any of the letters of the word 'mackerel'.

P53   In the south-east corner of Trafalgar Square in a cylindrical structure bearing a huge globe light on top. There is room for one policeman inside.

P64   Charing Cross, from where all distances are now measured

P70   It is a corridor in the Royal Courts of Justice. The origin of the nickname is not hard to deduce.

P83   It is the name of the largest bell in the clock room of St Paul's Cathedral; Big Ben is the name of the largest bell in St Stephen's Tower in the Palace of Westminster.

P99   Waterloo & City: because it names the only two stations that it serves, which are Waterloo and Bank (in the City)

P109 Lord Byron, on the house where he was born in Holles Street

P112 Mansion House and South Ealing

P122 William Shakespeare

P128 Livingstone

P136 Because eight feet were lost in a storm in 1764.

P140 They are the streets that are most frequently landed on on the Monopoly board.

FURTHER READING

The Absolutely Essential Guide to London,
David Benedictus

Capital Disasters, John Withington

*The Very Best of the Daily Telegraph Books of
Obituaries,* edited by Hugh Massingberd

Do Not Pass Go, Tim Moore

Eccentric London, Benedict le Vay

Footprint Guide to London, Charlie Godfrey-Faussett

A Literary Guide to London, Ed Glinert

Location London, Mark Adams

The London Compendium, Ed Glinert

Mysterious Britain, Janet and Colin Bord

The Nicholson London Pub Guide

Old Customs and Ceremonies of London,
Margaret Brentnall

Permanent Londoners, Judi Culbertson and Tom Ran

Subterranean City, Antony Clayton

Secret London, Andrew Duncan

The Penguin Dictionary of British Place Names,
Adrian Room

Top 10 of Everything 2004, Russell Ash

What's In A Name, Cyril M Harris

Walking Notorious London, Andrew Duncan

Encyclopedia of London Crime and Vice,
Fergus Linnane

The London Nobody Knows, Geoffrey Fletcher

London's Disused Underground Stations, JE Connor

NOTES, THOUGHTS AND JOTTINGS

NOTES, THOUGHTS AND JOTTINGS

NOTES, THOUGHTS AND JOTTINGS

NOTES, THOUGHTS AND JOTTINGS

NOTES, THOUGHTS AND JOTTINGS

NOTES, THOUGHTS AND JOTTINGS

NOTES, THOUGHTS AND JOTTINGS

NOTES, THOUGHTS AND JOTTINGS

NOTES, THOUGHTS AND JOTTINGS

NOTES, THOUGHTS AND JOTTINGS

NOTES, THOUGHTS AND JOTTINGS

NOTES, THOUGHTS AND JOTTINGS

NOTES, THOUGHTS AND JOTTINGS

NOTES, THOUGHTS AND JOTTINGS

CAPITAL THANKS

This book would not have been possible
without the painstaking research, cracking ideas,
and dogged support of:

Dominic Bates, Paul Bates, Adam Biles, Sarah Bove,
Anna Crane, Stuart Fance, Kim Gifford, Lucy Grewcock,
Ivo Grigorov, Lisa Holm, Nikki Illes, Iain, Suzie, Anne
and Niall Jenkins, Rachel Kurzfield, Charli Morgan,
Jennifer Style, Nathalie Stahelin, and Iain, Angela,
Alastair and Julie Swinnerton.

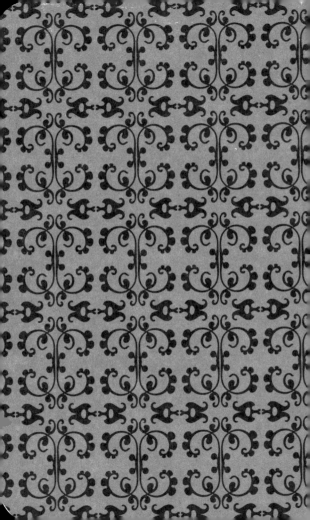